# Hey, Little Girl

# Hey, Little Girl

by

Vania Swain

# DEDICATION

*This book is dedicated to the younger me and the Little Girl inside of you. Hey, Little Girls, you are fearless, you are brave, and you are enough!*

*This book is also dedicated to my daughter, Kaira. You are a promise from God. My hope is that you will always be courageous enough to live life fully and dance to your own heartbeat.*

# CONTENTS

*When we deny our stories, they define us. When we own our stories, we get to write the ending.*
-Brené Brown

# INTRODUCTION

"HEY, LITTLE GIRL..." IS A past, present, and future approach to addressing negative labels. Oftentimes, we adopt an image of ourselves that a parent, caregiver, or societies' systems designed for us and we tend to get energetically stuck by those childhood labels. Those former labels travel with us into adulthood. Just like a piece of mail ending at the wrong address, if mislabeled, we can end up at the wrong destination feeling torn, misused, and lost.

This book is for women who want to not limit themselves from past labels and want to flow into their truest identity. If the abusive behavior of others from your past still weighs heavily on you and you want to learn to filter out any feelings of guilt, blame and shame, then come take this journey with me. If you are tired of living up to others' perceptions of you, then this book is for you. If you are done with being penalized for a snapshot in history instead of being seen as a beautiful picture that is still in the development process, you are in luck! If you are a woman who no longer wants permission to just BE, then keep on reading.

On the other hand, if you are a woman who is not ready to B.E., or not interested in doing the work to acquire inner peace, this book is not for you. If there is no interest in exploring, defining, and embracing your super-powers within, you're more than likely not going to resonate or connect with the contents of this book. The book you're holding in your hand is designed to help you see the best you, but if the old you is what you want more, then you can put the book down or give it to another woman who is ready for this transformative journey.

Why? This is the question I received a lot when it came to writing this book. Yes, the topic sounds like a relevant one, but why go through the process and the work it takes to publish this book, Vania? Because I could not stop thinking about you. I've prayed for all women who may feel stuck or like they are somewhere in the middle of nowhere. But the relentless nagging feeling I felt within convinced me that thinking, and praying wasn't enough.

I wrote this book because the Little Girl within needs your undivided attention. The reason you may feel unworthy, unseen, unheard, or even self-sabotage is because your

Little Girl is fearful of being hurt again. The Little Girl in you, needs reassurance and maybe a little re-parenting to let her know that she is now safe, loved, supported, and valued. The Little Girl still believes the negative names she was called, the feelings of being ignored, and how it feels to be compared to others and never being enough.

My sole purpose for writing this book is to push you from the strongholds of your past into the freedom of your future. Freeing yourself will give you the conviction you need to live limitless. If you unlock the door to a captured caged bird, that bird will fly to the highest heights and never look back. If this same bird has never tasted freedom, it will be complacent to stay in its cage. I'm here to let you know that freedom awaits you and you DESERVE it! I wrote this book as a way to use your wings to soar into your true identity—the sky's the limit for us all!

I understand that some of us deal with fear of "heights" when it comes to soaring in your purpose. I know how it feels to be haunted by doubts, fears, and shame. I have helped friends who felt emotionally paralyzed; their negative inner voice was reading the negative label that was put on them during their youth. I have witnessed clients transform as they peeled back the painful labels and realized the limitless potential of writing their own story. I have witnessed women let go of how they were conditioned to be and embrace who they are at their beautiful core. These women went through a 10-step system called the Delabeling Process and are now dancing to their own heartbeats. I believed it for them, and I believe it for you!

Allowing yourself to go back to identify your childhood labels can be a triggering process. If you feel yourself getting overwhelmed at any point, please reach out to a confidant, your coach, or therapist to walk through the process with you. *(Please see the list of Mental Health Resources in the rear of this book if needed).*

I did the work and was brave enough to believe bigger so I could become the best version of myself. I was once only inspired by transformational giants such as Lisa Nicolas to use my voice or motivated by Ilyana Vanzant to go from victim to victorious. But I was tired of learning about how to change, I wanted to live a changed life. I am now climbing the mountain of self-love as a Delabeled Woman who is reaching back to encourage you to take another step upward toward change.

This book is proof of my liberation. As you read, you will know that using my voice was the last thing I thought possible for me. Now, I use my voice to nurture the Little Girl within and to speak a liberated life into you.

Hey, Little Girl… Hey, Dear Reader… Let's journey to **Y**our Elevated **S**elf!

# HEY THERE!

Here is information on how to read this book…

*Hey, Little Girl…* will journey you through a ten step system using the Delabeling Process to help you peel back labels that have prevented your true authentic self from shining through. Most of us do not know our unique capabilities or as I like to call it our "super-powers." We all have them. But in order to tap into our super-powers we have to kill the ANTs (Automatic Negative Thoughts) derived from negative labels.

This book is divided into three sections.

**Section I**: The Labeled Girl is to help you understand what labels are, unveil the lies and embrace the truth of labels, and help you navigate forgiveness to absolve yourself and others.

**Section II**: The Peeled Girl will not only take off past labels, but also throw away any mask she's been wearing, learn how to just B.E. (Become and Evolve), learn how to focus on you without permission or apology, and help women to formulate a fleet of S.H.I.Ps to help strengthen her inner purpose.

**Section III**: The Liberated Girl will feel amazing for you but may be a shock to others. The chapters in this section will teach you how to reintroduce yourself in a healthy way, teach you the important differences between relapse and reset, and challenge you to live in your Y.E.S.

Each chapter starts with a story or illustration that expounds on the steps of the Delabeling Process. The Delabeling Process is comparable to an eaglet going from the shell to soaring. The eaglet may be seen as not exercising what it was born with initially, but once it starts to get the courage to leap and flap its wings, it will learn lessons on how to flow with the wind and become stronger as it comes into its own effortless glide.

After my personal reflections, you will see bolded greetings, "Hey, Little Girl." This is where I address my inner Little Girl. My desire to share the Little Girl within is to ensure that she is seen, heard, and loved—the way she has always needed to be. I want to reassure her that we have used our pain for our purpose. I want to pull the Little Girl in close, wrap my arms around her, and calm her fears. "Hey, Little Girl" is a gentle way to ask permission to look into the Little Girl's eyes and let her know that she is now safe. Reassuring the Little Girl within is one way I have found to heal childhood trauma. If you do not know exactly how this works, keep reading and use my interactions with my Little Girl as a conversation starter with your inner Little Girl.

You will also see a section called, "Hey, Dear Reader," that's me talking to you. The "Hey" is an amicable way to invite your attention to have one-on-one interaction with me. Even though we do not know one another personally, the fact that you are reading this book makes you near and dear to my heart. My heart wants nothing more than to witness other women like myself pulling down the walls that blocked them for far too long. The "Dear Reader," part is where you can take what is presented and apply it to your life.

At the end of each chapter there will be an interactive "Delabeling Exercise" to build your confidence to become your authentic you. As you journey through these pages, you will see that each chapter is a building block for the next in order to release you from the labeled into an elevated.

Before we dive into this journey, you might be wondering: Why did Vania Swain have to write this book? The reason is because I have been through the steps of the Labeled Girl, The Peeled Girl, and am living with my Liberated Girl. In a therapy session, two years ago, my therapist took me through an unexpected process called the Empty Chair Exercise which changed my life.

# Part 1: THE LABELED GIRL

worthless
mistake
slow
werïd
lonely

# CHAPTER 1: THE EMPTY CHAIR EXERCISE

*"Hurt must be heard before it is healed."*

-Pastor Michael Phillips

I WAS NERVOUS TO TALK to my therapist. She knew some incredibly secretive things about me, but what I needed to share that day with her was bound to make even her confused. She would recommend a psych evaluation for sure.

As I pulled up to the tall executive building where my therapist office was located, I felt mousy and a bit embarrassed. I looked at the building for about two minutes counting the windows as a distraction. Then, the blue light on the dashboard caught my eye … 2:55pm … it was time to go in. For some reason, I was weighed down with despair. I was able to confide a lot of deep secrets, past traumas, family situations, and personal stuff with my therapist. But, that day, I put her in the category with everyone else. When I share something "usual" for me with others, I can sometimes see the confusion on their faces or the "Oh, ok?" which is a nice translation for, "Girl, what in the world are you talking about?" With what I had to share, I did not think I would be fully understood, but what I had to share needed to come out.

The sound of the elevator ding interrupted my ruminating thoughts. I stepped out, walked around the corner, and looked down the long hall. It was about ten feet of hallway. Ten feet of anxiety building up with each step. Gripping my purse made my hands hurt, but it was a good way to focus on something else rather than on how I was about to humiliate myself in front of the only person I did not feel like I had to have a filter with.

I opened the brown shiny door and slowly walked inside with a fake smile to hide the fear that made my face hot enough to start perspiration on my forehead. As I walked from the waiting area to the therapist office, I glimpsed at a hanging vertical banner with the words, "Selah, tranquility, peace." I smiled as if someone verbalized those words to me and held on to them to keep me focused on the mission at hand … releasing.

My therapist, Dr. Sharon, was an African American

full-figured woman who wore an inviting smile. She always placed her hands in her lap and gave eye contact with her head cocked to the side as if to let me know that she was ready to dive in. If I were to pause or complete what I wanted to share, she would lean forward a bit with her elbow on each arm of the chair, cock her head to the other side, and give a warm smile as if to say, "Tell me more." Granted, I was paying for her expertise at the time, but my therapist made me feel like she was not only interested in me but invested in every word that came out of my mouth. I felt safe with her. And her red velvet chair with cozy throws across the arms of the love seat made me feel comfortable and at home. The electric waterfall was a great accent to the room and kept the atmosphere calm. And the smell of sweet almond essential oil made my senses at ease.

Even though I was on edge that day, when I sat on the comfy chocolate brown couch and looked at my therapist's face, I reverted to a Little Girl receiving assurance from a loving mom in a nerve-racking situation that it was going to be all right.

*"I don't know how to say this without sounding crazy"* was the first thing I said when I rested on the couch. I explained that there has been a recurring image that started popping up in my head over the last few years. It was a Little Girl who was sitting on the floor, knees to chest with her arms wrapped around her legs and her head rested in the circle

of her arms. She was wearing a dingy beige dress with holes scattered throughout. There was a sad eerie abandonment feeling that rested on her in a dim shallow place. I expressed that she comes to me at various times, but mostly when I am feeling upset by something. But lately, even when I am fine, she shows up unexpectedly causing me to take on the depression that she brings. Then, I turned to the therapist and said, "*I think the Little Girl is me.*"

Dr. Sharon put a black folding chair parallel to where I was sitting on the couch. "*I want you to do something today. It is called the **Empty Chair Exercise**. This exercise is used to help you reach and communicate with that Little Girl. I think she needs to talk to you about something and maybe you need to talk to her. Try to visualize you as a Little Girl, the age where she felt trapped. Then, I want you to talk to her and say whatever is on your heart. After you talk to the Little Girl, allow her to talk to you and anyone who has hurt her.*" She then gestured for a reply of understanding, and said, "*Are you ready?*" I looked at the chair and looked back at her thinking, *I am not the crazy one in this room, today, huh?*

I repeated the instructions to ensure I understood what I was about to agree to. "Sooooo you want me to talk to the empty chair, then talk to myself?" My therapist gracefully clasped her hands in her lap and repeated, "*I want you to talk to your Little Girl.*"

I closed my eyes and a waterfall of tears cascaded down

my face. It did not take long before the Little Girl's image appeared sitting in the chair where the therapist instructed her to be. I could not find the words to say. As I was energetically pulled closer to her, the darker the room seemed to become. My surroundings were suddenly quiet. I knelt down beside her and whispered, *"Hey, Little Girl, I am sorry. I am sorry that I ignored you for so long. I didn't know what to do with you… I just wanted you to stop showing up in my head. But all you wanted is my attention and now you have it.*

*"I am sorry that you are so sad. The things that happened were not your fault. I understand why you felt so lonely. I know the bullying at home was confusing, scary, and hurtful. I can see how not fitting in made you feel lost and unwanted. You didn't want to be a bother, so you held so much in, suffering alone … but I am here for you now, Little Girl.*

*"I see you, I feel your pull and now I am here. I am so sorry it took me so long. You are so strong and pushed through a lot of hard stuff that was not meant for a kid to handle, but you did it. I think you are amazing, Little Girl. I love you … you were always lovable. You were always beautiful. You were always enough."*

As I poured my heart out in tears and with a quivering voice, I saw the image of the Little Girl slowly lift her head up and look me in my eyes. I always had a feeling that the Little Girl was me, but I never saw her face. The Little Girl was me, but not only me. She somehow looked like every Little Girl I had seen throughout my life. Remember, I told you this was going to sound crazy!

The doctor's voice interrupted my trance and said, "Now, let the Little Girl talk to you."

The Little Girl went from seated position to standing. She looked at me intently and then looked around as if she saw something behind me. She then smiled. In a youthful voice, the Little Girl spoke: *"Wow, look at you! You are so beautiful. I really like your husband; he is nice. And your daughter, she looks like me! I am glad you have great friends who treat you kindly. You have so much fun with them. I didn't want to bother you, but I needed you. I wanted to be with you. I am so proud of you! I am proud of all the lessons you have learned and never stopped trying. I am glad you didn't give up when you felt really sad that time… I am glad we are still here."*

"Does she have anything to say to anyone else?" my therapist asked.

The Little Girl looked straight forward as if she was looking at a sea of people. *"I forgive you. I understand. I am ok now!"*

I looked up at her as she stood with confidence. The area in my mind began to illuminate and I stood up in front of her with tears flowing … this time these were happy tears. I felt myself smiling.

*"What is she doing now?"* the therapist inquired.

I opened my eyes. As I attempted to adjust to the light in the room, I saw a moving image flowing back and forth throughout the room. I went from smiling to laughing while wiping the tears that were still pouring from my eyes. I followed the Little Girl who now had a long flowy iridescent dress on. With every swing and sway the colors of the rainbow followed her like a dance partner. When my therapist finally caught my eyes, I blurted out, *"THE LITTLE GIRL IS DANCING!"*

**Hey, Little Girl:** You have been stuck for so long, what made you get up and dance?

**Hey, Dear Reader:** What happens next? Turn the page. The Delabeling Process starts now...

# CHAPTER 2:
# IDENTIFYING LABELS

## (Step One of the Delabeling Process)

*"I think putting labels on people is just an easy way of marketing something you don't understand."*

– ADAM JONES

I LEFT THE OFFICE AS light as a feather … literally skipping down the long hall that led to the elevator. As I waited for the elevator to arrive, I closed my eyes and started swaying. There she was, dancing to her own heartbeat … twirling in a light blue dress with lace and frills, arms swinging freely in the air, and a smile that was big enough to light up South Jersey. My smile matched her smile. A child-like unrefined giggle blurted out from pure joy. I covered my mouth and began to laugh hysterically until the elevator doors opened. The person that stepped out of that elevator was not the same person who stepped in two hours ago. No, I felt empty of shame, free of blame, and released from guilt. I remember thinking, *I don't know the last time I felt this way,* as I looked around the empty elevator. My eyes caught my reflection from the shiny stainless steel. I looked at myself, and whispered, *"I love you!"*

The ding sound of the elevator broke my intimate time with me. It felt a little awkward because I never said, *"I love you,"* to myself before. At the same time, saying those words felt perfectly normal and for the first time, I only thought about me like a girl may daydream about a cute boy she had a crush on. It felt good. When I sat in my car, I began to replay everything that just happened. Then a simple thought popped in my head. *"Why were you stuck for so long, Little Girl?"*

As I thought about how my Little Girl was stuck in the same position for so long, times where I got stuck in life simultaneously began to surface. I remembered not feeling qualified at the age of seventeen for a shift manager position when I worked at McDonalds, even though I worked every position for the last two years. I remember secretly feeling like an imposture when I was promoted at Bank of America from line teller to teller supervisor. I initially declined the offer, then accepted with some convincing from my bank manager. Another time, as a matron of honor at my former best friend's reception, I remember declining the request to say a toast because I was terrified that I would stutter over my words; I never felt that I had a voice or could articulate well and I did not want to embarrass my bestie on her day.

So, while I left the therapist's office unburdened, I also left realizing that occurrences from my childhood struck fear in me on many occasions. But why? Why was my Little Girl stuck for so long and why have I been stuck in many areas of my life as an adult? The real question I needed to answer was, *"Why did my Little Girl get up?"* My Little Girl shifted her position from sitting to standing when I started peeling back those negative labels she held onto for so long.

It was the labels!

Omgness ... *"I wonder what labels I have stuck on me?"*

**Hey, Little Girl:** Because of a moment in time, someone gave you a life sentence via labels. The silly nicknames, the jokes, the little "slights" all made a stamp in your thought process and behavior. I understand why you believed these labels to be true. The most important people in your life believed certain things about you that were negative, so it had to be true, right?

Wrong, it's not true. I believe deep inside, even at a young age, you knew it wasn't true either. That is why you would not move from your position and that's why you were trying to get my attention. Well, you have it now,

Little Girl. To see you go from stuck to dancing broke a chain in me and freed me from judgements of our past. Hey, Little Girl, you are so brave.

**Hey, Dear Reader:** The first step in the Delabeling Process is Identifying the Labels.

## WHAT ARE CHILDHOOD LABELS?

Childhood labels are core beliefs developed by the way someone perceives you early in life. The labels that impacted you at a young age oftentimes follow you into adulthood. For this book, childhood labels are defined as strongholds that keep you stuck and stagnant from reaching goals, facing new challenges, and embodying your unique identity. Anything from the career path you chose, the friends you have, and the beliefs you have may all be linked to labels from the past. Even subconsciously, our adult behaviors reflect what we experienced in our childhood.

When you operate with childhood labels, you see yourself in a certain light that impacts the way you feel about yourself and how you portray yourself to other people. Labels are limiting. Interest, activities, passions, and purpose are oftentimes unfilled because childhood labels are still stifling us.

Labels are formed when verbal, physical, or mental

attacks are consistent. As a child, we start to believe and conform to others' direct or indirect opinions of us. We allow negative words to penetrate our souls and take it on as our identity. Our impressionable years were the time when we soaked up good and bad habits, thoughts, and behaviors like a sponge. During this vulnerable time, we are susceptible to taking on labels that influence us throughout our life without knowing. Things that you are exposed to, such as verbal insults, on a consistent basis become a part of you. You begin to believe what people say and think of you especially if you do not have anyone to protect you from harmful language. Little by little, words start to stick and manifest through your conduct. Because of a snapshot in time, you now serve a lifetime sentence with the penalty of labels.

## HOW DO YOU KNOW IF YOU ARE LABELED?

You know you are labeled when there is a constant reoccurring of unwanted and unexplained behavior. Some label imprints are subtle, but still cause noticeable damage with us, mentally and in other relationships. Sherrie Hurd, creative writer for *Mental Minds*, highlighted seven subtle displays of childhood labels that may be seen through:

- Passive behavior as an adult because you were neglected as a child.

- Passive-aggressive behavior due to witnessing anger

or suppressing anger as a child.

- Adults that experience depression and anxiety due to bullying as a child.

- Physical health problems caused from mental health problems.

- Defensiveness due to experiencing extreme stress as a child.

- Creating a false personality through people pleasing to receive the love desired.

- Victim mentality because of being victimized as a child; adults often get stuck in a victim mindset.

These seven subtle behaviors are only a few signs that you are labeled. It is critical to become aware of your personal childhood experience and how it has left its mark on your life. If you can identify with any of the subtle displays, the Delabeling Process will serve you well with uprooting toxic behavior patterns that you no longer desire. This practical process was formulated to help you fully peel-off unwanted childhood labels to walk in your truest identity.

## I'M LABELED, NOW WHAT (IT'S A STICKY SITUATION)?

Transformation by peeling off childhood labels can be a sticky process. While I do not prescribe to dwell on past hurts and traumas, taking a brief look back to understand what labels are orchestrating your life is helpful.

On one hand, allowing yourself to go back to identify your childhood labels can be a triggering process. If you feel yourself getting overwhelmed at any point, please reach out to a confidant, your coach, or therapist to walk through the process with you. *(Please see the list of Mental Health Resources in the rear of this book)*. On the other hand, taking a look back to see what labels are attached can bring self-awareness. That is the main purpose of this section.

Self-awareness increases knowledge of who you are right now. When you are able to understand the present self, you are able to evaluate your thoughts and emotions better. When you are able to evaluate your thoughts and emotions, you will likely get curious about the origin of your thoughts and emotions. When you dig deep into the origin of your thoughts and emotions, you will realize patterns of behavior and cognition. Patterns of behavior and cognition lead straight back to routines and habits you became accustomed to from your youth. See how that works? Self-awareness is not an easy task, but it is so valuable when identifying childhood labels. Acknowledging how one little word or phrase influenced your core beliefs might help you gain more insight into yourself and the choices you've made.

When you are self-aware, you are able to identify behavioral patterns that you are not fond of. We all have things we say and do and then wonder why we reacted a certain way. We will get frustrated with ourselves, not even fully understanding our emotional triggers. And so we do not have to deal with the uncomfortable feeling longer than desired, we get annoyed with ourselves, project it onto someone else or dismiss the feeling altogether. But it always resurfaces.

Self-awareness to identify past labels helps a great deal. As you dig deep the next question that surfaces is: "Why?" Why was I labeled in the first place? In the next chapter, we will unveil the lies and embrace the truth about our past labels.

# CHAPTER 3: UNVEILING THE LIES AND EMBRACING THE TRUTH

**(Step Two of the Delabeling Process)**

*"The truth is like a scalpel. The truth is painful, because it opens all of the wounds which are covered by lies so that we can be healed."*
–Don Miguel Ruiz

I DID NOT FEEL ANY pain until I saw the blood on my hand. I remember hearing the crack from the bat hitting the ball and knew it was my time to shine! I ran toward the base made out of torn cardboard boxes to score the winning point for my team. Somehow sliding into the base ended up being a trip and falling over my left foot and a crash landing on my right leg. I dusted my leg off, then went to dust what I thought was dirt off my hands. I glanced down for a second and saw blood smeared across my hands. When I peered at my leg, I screamed, not because I was in pain, but because there was a gash so deep, I thought I saw my fibula bone.

That night at the hospital I heard the nurse say, "It's only gonna be a few stitches but we have to get the glass out first." She pulled out a long needle to numb the bruised area. I immediately started panting and pleaded that she leave the glass in and allow it to heal over time.

You see, I wanted to take the least painful way possible and experience healing that wouldn't leave a scar. But I learned from that hospital experience that detrimental things which are not removed will only make wounds worse and the process of healing longer. I had to suck it up and allow them to clean out everything that could potentially cause me more harm in the future.

## HEALING FROM EMOTIONAL WOUNDS WAS MUCH HARDER.

"Skinny-mini, Bonezilla, the Lollipop Kid, Tit-toe-bittie, goody two shoe, and suck-up…" My brother was very creative when it came to giving me a new nickname. I was one of eight … the oldest girl and a middle child. I had three older brothers and after I was born my father was on cloud nine. His prayers were finally manifested. He would always remind me every chance he got that he prayed for me to have long beautiful hair as well as be loving and loved by others … so glad prayer works! I could do no wrong in his eyes, but that did not stop my siblings from proving my father wrong.

The attention I was getting as a baby took attention away from my older brothers. My third brother, in particular, had a hard time not being the youngest anymore. I can only imagine that as a three year-old, his first thought was: *'Who was this brown-skinned, brown-eyed little baby with a head full of curly hair taking up all of the affection and attention?'* To him, I must've been a rude awakening stealing the spotlight. Whatever he was thinking about his new baby sister could not have been good and he made sure I knew just how unhappy he was with me being in the picture every chance he had. Even after my four younger siblings were born, I felt like his number one target and he practiced on me every chance he had.

The labels my brother placed on me did not stick initially because, as they say, "Boys will be boys," and sibling rivalry was normal in our home. The escalations of teasing went from physical assaults to actions that were inimical to my emotional and mental state. I began to see myself as "skinny mini," so over time, instead of knee length skirts, I started wearing maxi skirts and dresses so no one would see my bony legs. I didn't want to be a "goody two shoes," so I would be the one to steal the sugar from the cupboard when we made mud pies in the yard. I didn't want to be called "tit-toe bittie," so I stole my mother's bra and stuffed it with tissue to show that I was budding like my peers. That is one of my biggest regrets because my brother did not let me live that down for months.

It's funny because I never thought anything was wrong with me until repetitive reminders of how awful I looked and how much he abhorred me became a daily, and seemingly bi-hourly occurrence. When my brother was able to get the other siblings on board, the "terrorize tit-toe-bittie" tour started, and it sealed their perception of me as truth.

When I was about eight, my older brother positioned five of the siblings on the couch on one side of a rectangle glass coffee table and I knelt on the opposite side on the carpet. He then told my younger sister, the sixth sibling, to sit between his legs in the same kneeling position I was in. He commanded her to punch me in the face, but she refused, looking confused and fearful at the same time. When I heard his orders, I was puzzled as well. What is he up to now? He then grabbed my sister's arm, folded her fingers together to make a fist, pulled her arm back, and came full force into my face. I do not remember feeling pain right away, but I do remember hearing a hollow ringing sound between my ears. I looked at my sister and simultaneously our eyes began to water, then I looked down at my shirt, which was decorated in blood. I grabbed my nose in an attempt to stop the bleeding and jumped back to escape from another potential punch.

With every tear and drip of blood, out came my dignity, trust, belonging, and understanding of how true friendship works. That day, I physically left that kneeling position, but my eight year old Little Girl was energetically stuck at that coffee table and has been for thirty-one years.

## THE REPLAY OF THAT SCENE WAS LIKE A BROKEN RECORD.

We had a record player growing up. I loved listening to good ole hymnals from gospel singers like Mahalia Jackson and James Cleveland. When they were scratched or broken, it was annoying. As soon as you get to the good part of the song, it starts skipping and repeating the words in the broken part. That's the feeling I had with replaying the "me against the world" scene. My family was my world and seeing my siblings on one side and me on the other made me feel unsafe in many other relationships growing up.

Dr. Sharon thought the Empty Chair Exercise would help me because my mental record was scratched. I was able to push the pause button with distraction, but when I settled in a happy space, that scene would play again, and again, and again just like a scratched record.

# I NEEDED TO GRAB HOLD OF WHAT WAS TRUE IN ORDER TO SURVIVE.

The truth is, my siblings and I witnessed a lot of physical, emotional, and mental abuse growing up. My brother was projecting a feeling of neglect as a child onto me. The lack of positive attention from my father, my mother being preoccupied with the other children, and being bullied in school were all pinned up frustrations that my brother released onto me.

Sibling aggression is oftentimes more mentally suppressive than any other type of bullying.

When you live with the person that terrorizes you on a day to day basis, there is no escape. The cruelty of a sibling is traumatizing mostly because it is experienced on a consistent basis and the heart remembers what the brain tries to forget. The emotions that are attached to past hurts resurfaced in future encounters. It felt the same but was not the same situation. This was a recurring theme for me throughout my life and I needed to learn how to navigate the pain. Most of all, I knew I wanted to be free from the imprisonment of my past labels.

Grabbing hold to the truth like a perry-buoy to keep from drowning is what rescued my self-worth. Embracing the truth was the start of letting go of labels that were a negative dictator in my life. Questions like, "Why was I being targeted? How come my brother didn't get the memo to my dad's answered prayer? What was so wrong with me? And why was I hated so much?" were never answered, so my Little Girl stayed buried under a pile of labels with no resolve. The assumption of my past drew conclusions that I am unwanted, I am hated, I don't belong, I am ugly, I am friendless, and I will always be lonely. These are the labels that stuck to me, but I now realize these were all lies. The reality was I experienced a scientifically proven misfortune called sibling aggression. Focusing on this truth not only helped me release my sadness but opened the door to forgiveness for my brother as well. The truth cultivated a greater understanding of empathy for us both.

**Hey, Little Girl**: Somehow you managed to survive peer bullying, but the sibling aggression you experienced took a toll on you. The truth is that your brother grew to love you. Oftentimes, people have to work through their own issues before coming to grips with how their behavior affects others. Before he passed away, your brother apologized to you and your relationship was reconciled. Though you have forgiven him, you had to work through the residue even after taking off the labels. I am so grateful that this journey of Delabeling freed both of us from our childhood strongholds. Now that we do not have to listen to the broken record of the past, we can now flow in the euphonious rhythm of our future.

You have also learned the true meaning of empathy, for empathy is seeing with the eyes of another, listening with the ears of another, and feeling with the heart of another. I empathize with you, Little Girl. Now, you know the truth, and the truth has set you free.

**Hey, Dear Reader:** Unveiling lies is like Dorothy pulling back the curtains on "The Great and Powerful Oz." The intimidating wizard was obnoxiously loud, belittling, and menacing to all because he feared his true adversary, the Wicked Witch of the West. But he took his fears out on a Lion who wanted to find his courage, a Tin Man who desired a heart, a Scarecrow who needed a brain, and Dorothy who desperately wanted to find her way home. The truth of the matter was The Great and Powerful Oz was not so great. He projected his fear and authoritarian demands onto people who needed him most.

THE TRUTH IS HURT PEOPLE HURT PEOPLE; however, that is how pain patterns persist from person to person and generation to generation. Taking responsibility for our own healing advances the truth from a proverb that hurt people hurt people, to whole people heal people. When Dorothy confronted Oz for his behavior, she realized that he was just as terrified as everyone else was. Despite Oz's shortcomings, she did not allow him to continue to hold her in contempt. She was able to help find a solution for everyone, including Oz, to get what they traveled so far for by no longer giving power to Oz's imposture mentality. Instead, she shifted the power back to her purpose which was journeying toward her destination.

Finding out the truth behind your labels does not make excuses for them, it gives explanations about them. Like Oz, my brother projected his feelings outward to feel some sense of empowerment inwardly. Labeling people does not empower but serves as a temporary fix to a broken and frightened soul. Embracing the truth that lies underneath the labels is a step in discovering the truest form of you.

THE LIE IS THAT THE LABEL IS TRUE. Past labels stick because at some point we internalized the labels as fact instead of someone's opinion or perception. Once we recognize it in our adulthood, however, the challenge is sorting through the lie and the truth of the label. The truth is, labels come by projections, jealousy, or a moment in time.

Lisa Nicholas was labeled a terrible public speaker by her teacher. She shared that her teacher advised her to never speak in public again. Today she is one of the most renowned transformational speakers, author of four best-selling books, and an "auntie" to all who are inspired to live at their fullest potential by ripping off limiting labels.

Jim Kwik was marked as "the boy with a bad brain" even though his injury caused his inability to learn as fast as his peers. He is now an international brain coach, motivational speaker, and author teaching people how to unlock their brain power to live limitlessly.

And let's not forget Maya Angelou, a woman who was ridiculed as a child as well as becoming voiceless because of the guilt she felt for protecting herself from a predator who was killed for his crime. She found her voice in poetry and defied past labels, inspiring people across the nation to embrace the fullness of who they are.

People will try to give you a life sentence because of a moment in time, but there are examples of people who unveiled the lies of their past and embraced the truth of their true selves … and you can, too!

I shared my story of how I became stuck by past labels, now it's time for you to share yours. Taking a mental glance into the origin of your labels is an important part of the Delabeling Process. When you are able to get to the root of your labels, you are able to pull up and pull out the strongholds that are buried so deep within. This step is a painful part of the process, but it is a necessary one. David Richo assures, "Our wounds are often the openings into the best and most beautiful part of us." Trust the process and let's explore the beauty that lives in you.

## Delabeling Exercise

This exercise is to help you unveil the lies of your labels and embrace the truth of who you really are now.

1. List three labels that limit you. Leave 5 lines between each label. (Ex. Unintelligent, Unloved, Lonely, etc.)
2. Write down the origin of the labels on the second line. (Ex. The label was given by my 5th grade teacher.)
3. What is the lie? Write one lie on third line. (Ex. "you are not smart")
4. What is the truth of behind why you were labeled? Write two truths on the fourth and fifth line. (Ex. I am educated and growing in Emotional Intelligence and Relational Intelligence every day. I am a life learner and growing in wisdom.)

Once you have finished read each label, lie and truths. Reread, but this time erase the lie. Embrace and internalize your truth because this is who you really are!

### <u>I just want you to know:</u>

Some traumatizing offenses are more heinous than others. I shared my experience to help you see the value of unveiling and embracing the truth of how and why past limiting labels can become crippling and a disruption throughout adulthood. Please seek additional help from a trusted friend, your professional therapist, or coach to help you walk through these steps if it becomes an overwhelming exercise. Remember to be patient with yourself … this is a process.

# CHAPTER 4: THE PROCESS OF FORGIVENESS

## (Step Three of the Delabeling Process)

*"Forgiveness is key because we are fighting something way bigger."*

—Beyoncé

IN MY LAST YEAR OF my undergrad, I took a course called, Positive Psychology. I was immediately interested in the course by the title alone. Within a three month span, I was introduced to ways to achieve well-being and how to flourish in life through PERMA (Positive Emotion, Engagement, Relationships, Meaning, and Achievement) self-assessments, and VIA (Values in Action) strength inventories. One of the assignments that was emotionally changing for me was the subject of forgiveness. I was just beginning my journey to self-healing, and forgiveness was always a subject I wrestled with. I was taught to "forgive and forget" and understood that to mean excusing people who have offended me and "getting over it." How I witnessed forgiveness growing up was always controversial in my mind. What if the person who caused the offense repeats the "crime," what if the person is not remorseful, what if the person does not truly see the depth of damage caused? How do I forgive what my heart will not let me forget?

For one of my assignments, we were challenged to expound on the importance of forgiveness. I automatically highlighted reasons for forgiving others first, because to me, forgiveness was not about the victim, but about giving the victimizer another chance, or so I thought. To my surprise, the first passage I read from my textbook was about forgiveness being a character strength of temperance.

> *Forgiveness is an act of having mercy, which tempers hatred and anger… true forgiveness goes a step further, offering empathy, compassion, and understanding toward the offender … forgiveness is both a virtue … when a person possesses temperance in the form of forgiveness, they are not retaliatory or act out excessively but display calmness, restraint from arrogance and humility remembering that forgiveness is a gift to the offender and will be hopefully reciprocated when needed.*

Forgiveness is a gift to the offender? I should hope that

it is reciprocated? For some reason, I wasn't ok with that. I have to accept the offense AND give the gift of forgiveness in return? What kind of imbalance teaching is this? (*Yes, I had an immediate attitude and rolled my eyes at the computer as if it could feel every piece of my wrath!*) This is the teaching I heard in church when the preacher would give a sermon on that faithful scripture about Jesus' commandment to "forgive seventy times seven." This is the message I internalized when my father would abuse my mother and somehow still be permitted to stay in the home. My understanding of some of the teachings and the dysfunctions I witnessed as a child concerning forgiveness always seemed one-sided.

As I delved deeper into my studies, I came across several scholarly articles and other professional literature highlighting the holistic benefits of forgiveness.

> *One of the personal benefits of forgiveness is psychological freedom ... people who forgive easily have lower levels of stress and people who ruminate and hold grudges have high levels of life-time stress ... forgiveness is emotional stability ... people who are forgiving tend to have higher levels of agreeableness and lower levels of neuroticism ... produces good physical health ... forgiveness diffuses chronic anger and helps regulate the heart rate, blood pressure and immune response ... forgiveness decreases the risk of depression, heart disease and diabetes, among other conditions ... as unforgiveness*

*negatively affects coronary circulation, forgiveness, however, has proved to calm stress levels, leading to improved health.*

I never viewed forgiveness in this way before. My focus was on the "give" part of forgiveness. I realized that I could keep that same focus but switch the energy inward. I needed to "give" to myself. For some reason at that moment, I was reminded of the message I delivered over ten years ago called 'Forgiveness Pays Off' during a Youth Church Service. During the sermon, I illustrated how unforgiveness was like chaining yourself to the neck of an offender. I shared the experience of my strained relationship with my father. Even during that time I did not understand the fullness of forgiveness, but I knew I was ready to find a way to break the chains that constrained us both.

The real reason I was having a hard time with the forgiveness assignment was because I cultivated an unbalanced view. In a desperate need to heal my wounds, I neglected important steps, which I now realize is why my Little Girl was so adamant to get my attention. Forgiving my past was not only about excusing the past labels from others but forgiving the ones I placed on myself. I realized that there is a process to forgiveness. First, I needed to forgive myself, then forgive others, and even without an apology, I owed it to myself to do the work. I owed my future self the opportunity to love and be loved completely by tearing off and releasing past labels that no longer applied to me.

**Hey, Little Girl:** "I forgive you," those words coming from you held more weight than ever before. You not only forgave others who labeled you, but you forgave me as well. What happened in our past, impacted our present. But, with forgiveness you were able to change your position from depressed to dancing, giving life to our future.

I have learned to dance to the beat of our own drum, too! I understand the process of forgiveness and live freer than I ever have. Thank you for forgiving me. Thank you for showing me how liberating it is to emancipate from the imprisonment of unforgiveness. Now, I help other women liberate their Little Girl, for what I see in us, I see in others.

**Hey, Dear Reader:** In theory, forgiveness is one of the best gifts you can extend to yourself and others to bring peace. Some offenses are harder to recover from than others. To learn the process of forgiveness, it is important to understand the misconceptions about forgiveness and to know what forgiveness is not. Dr. Andrea Brandt helps us understand that:

- Forgiveness does not mean excusing other's actions.

- Forgiveness does not mean you need to tell the person they are forgiven.

- Forgiveness does not mean there is nothing further to work out.

- Forgiveness does not mean that everything is ok, and you do not have other feelings to work out.

- Forgiveness does not mean forgetting the incident ever happened.

- Forgiveness does not mean you have to continue to include them in your life.

- Forgiveness is not something you do for the other person.

There is a process when forgiving yourself and others. Do not let anyone rush you into forgiveness; it is necessary for Delabeling yourself, but it also works in your own timing.

1. Accept what happened.
2. Acknowledge the hurt.
3. Process the pain.
4. Instill boundaries.
5. Release.

Though the process of forgiveness is tried and true, forgiveness will look different when it comes to forgiving yourself, forgiving others, forgiving without an apology, and forgiving without "receipts."

## FORGIVE YOURSELF

In your process of forgiveness, first forgive yourself. Past labels oftentimes blur the image of who we are at our core, but you have to remember that there is nothing wrong with you. You have patterns to unlearn, new behaviors to embody, and wounds to heal. You are unlearning generations of harm, so give yourself grace.

Forgive yourself for the hurts you have caused. Forgive yourself for the times you betrayed yourself to gain the approval of others. Forgive yourself for the times you were not 100 percent honest with how you deserved to be treated. Forgive yourself for not operating in your worth. Forgive yourself for doubting your gut time and time again. Forgive yourself because your Little Girl thinks you are deserving of another chance.

***Forgiveness is a form of self-care***. It is like opening the window to a stuffy house to air out any hostility within. As the enmity exits, a fresh breeze of tranquil energy enters, occupying spaces that need healing.

With every act of self-care your authentic self gets stronger and your ANTs (Automatic Negative Thoughts) will get weaker. You are able to show up for yourself with unconditional love and acceptance. Every act of self-care is a powerful declaration that I will celebrate the small triumphs and learn from the minor defeats.

In the midst of your forgiveness process, bestselling author and life coach, Iyanla Vanzant, encourages you to be yourself, accept yourself, trust yourself, empower yourself, bless yourself, value yourself, express yourself, love yourself, and forgive yourself! Forgiveness is your gift to you … take good care of you!

## FORGIVE OTHERS

By forgiving, you are accepting the reality of what happened and finding a way to live in a state of resolution with it. You may never fully comprehend why someone did you wrong, but with empathy and compassion you are still able to truly forgive. You will be able to walk in their shoes and understand why they operate in the way they do. It does not lessen the pain of your experience, but over time you will be able to walk through the process of forgiveness with the knowledge that, while you don't have control over others' actions, you have control over your response.

Other shoes will be too uncomfortable to try on. They will either be too small, where you realize their offense was purposeful or too big, meaning the trauma experienced was caused by brutal abuse or heinous wrongdoing. In these situations, ask yourself if you are willing to forgive. If you decide to forgive, apply the process of forgiving by accepting what happened, acknowledging the hurt, processing the pain, instilling boundaries, and releasing any remorse, hatred, guilt or shame attached to the incident. Take your time to work through your feelings, learn from what happened by acknowledging your growth, and honor yourself in your newfound liberation.

If you are not ready to forgive, it is ok. Do not allow anyone to rush you into forgiveness. Ponder on this excerpt from a book called HER by Pierre Alex Jeanty:

*Do not expect her to just get up and forgive. Have you known anyone who has been shot in the heart and didn't bleed or suffer from the pain it brings? To demand that she acts like it didn't hurt and put it easily in the past, is to ask her to be a robot, rather than a human who feels. Leave her to heal.*

Focus on healing yourself. When you are ready, entertain the thought of forgiving others and if you are able, start the process of forgiveness. You may not understand fully what forgiveness will do for you but know the process does not end with healing ... healing is just the beginning. The goal is to flourish in your destiny that is already yours for the taking!

## FORGIVENESS WITHOUT AN APOLOGY

A prerequisite for giving someone a second chance is that they are able to clearly articulate the growth they've had. Marriage and Family Therapist Vienna Pharaon posted a thought provoking Instagram message that read, "If they can't tell you what they've changed, and what their commitment is, the likelihood that you'll get stuck in the same pattern is high." It is easier to reconcile an offense with an apology. But what is the response when people attempt to engage with you without remorse? How can we accept and repeat the words of the Little Girl, "I forgive you. It is ok. I understand," without verbal recognition of harm done.

No one wants an apology that is offered in the form of manipulation to get back in good graces, or out of guilt for being caught red handed. This is futile; a waste of time. But, when someone says, "Please forgive me," from a sincere heart, it goes a long way to feeling recognized for pain caused. It softens a hard heart from animosity. Granted, offenses range on a spectrum of minor to extreme, but with an apology and real change, the violation may be a little easier to bear.

There are times when the offender will not feel sorry for a traumatic experience from childhood. If your parent's authoritarian parental style was a traumatic experience for you, more than likely the parent will not feel they have done any injustice if they believe they raised you the best way they could or they were doing the right thing.

As a child, many of us were raised as little people with no voice because of the belief that a child should be seen and not heard. Children were not allowed to respond or express themselves without the adult feeling like they disrespectfully talked back. "Staying in a child's place" is decoded as you do not have an opinion, you do not have feelings … be grateful, accept whatever I say, and stay out of the way.

From the previous chapter, we understand where this traditional mindset came from, but it came with labels that damaged many of us in adulthood. Now, that we are in this Delabeling Process, how do we truly forgive and no longer suppress limiting labels to become free? You cannot heal from suppressing hurts, you heal from releasing hurts.

Nancy Colier, from *Psychology Today,* explains that when hurt by another, our bodies are hard wired to need an apology to relax, move forward, and let go of the hurt. However, when an "I'm sorry" DOES NOT happen, knowing that your pain is deserving of kindness and trusting that your truth is justified and valid, you are able to begin your independent healing process of forgiveness. Without an apology, you can still get the love and reassurances you need from your support system or as I call it your "Fleet of S.H.I.Ps." We will touch on that in Chapter 8. Do what you have to do to forgive and move forward, seeking no approval from anyone but yourself.

## NO RETURN WITHOUT A RECEIPT

Every time you return something at the store, they ask for your receipt. A receipt is proof where the item is from, when the item was purchased, and what form of payment was received for the purchase. A receipt is like a golden ticket when it comes to returning unwanted items. Even without a receipt, if you were to return a blouse, the article of clothing cannot be worn, and the tag has to be attached. If you order the item online, now-a-days you can return items through the mail, but the item has to be returned in the same condition it was sent. The point is, there has to be some proof that the blouse is worthy of being returned, restocked, and resold.

A relationship that's on the mend should have the same process. If you have done the work to forgive yourself, forgive others, and even accepted that no apology will be given, then you need proof that the other person in the relationship did their work as well.

Evolving into your authentic you is work! When mending a relationship, reevaluate if the compatibilities are still there. When checking the "receipt," consider how the relationship is serving you.

Dr. Vienna Pharaon advised us to consider these questions when considering returns:

1.  Does this relationship expand me or serve me in any way?
2.  Is there both output and input happening in this dynamic that feels balanced?
3.  Is there reciprocity that is felt on both sides?
4.  What fears or stressors come up when I think

about navigating away from a relationship?

5. What story do I tell myself?

6. If I shift my expectations of this person, does anything change?

7. Is there something I can address with this friend to shed light in order to see if the dynamic might change?

Checking the receipts is an essential step in the forgiveness process not to instill unrealistic expectations, but to examine if the relationship can be returned to a healthy state for both parties. You can have unconditional love for yourself and others, but it does not mean the relationship has to be unconditional. There is no organic peace without forgiveness. So, forgive the toxic behaving people in your life, but deny them access to you. As a friend once said, "Forgiveness granted, access denied!"

**Hey, Dear Reader:** The concept of forgiveness is a lot to take in. Here is an exercise to sum up what you have learned and how to apply it now.

<table>
<tr><td align="center">Delabeling Exercise</td></tr>
<tr><td>

Let's Journal!

- How can you apply the forgiveness process to yourself?

- How can you apply the forgiveness process to someone else?

- How can you apply the forgiveness process to someone who has not apologized?

- How can I apply forgiveness to someone who cannot return without a receipt?

- How will forgiveness upgrade my life?"

</td></tr>
</table>

# Part II: THE PEELED GIRL

# CHAPTER 5: THE MASK

## (Step Four of the Delabeling Process)

*"Our need to be 'greater than' or 'less than' has been a defense against toxic shame. A shameful act was committed upon us. The perpetrator walked away leaving us with the shame. We absorbed the notion that we are somehow defective. To cover for this we constructed a false self. A masked self."*

—Maureen Brady

WARNING!! IT IS SO EASY to go from taking past labels off to putting on an emotional mask.

I remember watching a movie *The Mask* with Jim Carrey. His character, Stanley Ipkiss, was a bank clerk who was a shy guy that did not handle confrontation well. He was picked on by his boss, bullied by his landlady, and seemed to be jinxed when it came to romantic relationships. Even when he experienced love at first sight with a beautiful nightclub singer, he was repelled like a bug from entering because he did not look the part.

After a really bad day, he was on his way home when he crossed a mysterious mask in a pile of scraps. When he arrived home and pondered over the catastrophe of a day he had, he remembered the ancient mask he found.

When Ipkiss hesitatingly puts on the mask, the mask attaches itself to his face and turns him into this green-faced animation, which is his alter ego manic superhero. Throughout the movie, The Mask became a bank robber to fund his ventures, interfered in police investigations, which ended in a fatality for one of the officers, and caused mayhem throughout the city.

While Ipkiss wanted to help solve crime, he did not see himself as capable of doing it on his own. He was not enough. So he repeatedly attempted to make things right by reinventing himself through this false persona—but it only made things worse!

Masking will only make things worse!

Even though Ipkiss felt horrible after a night full of bizarre tricks that lead to fatalities, he wore the mask again. The Mask was the only way he would be accepted into the nightclub to see the girl of his dreams perform.

Needing acceptance can be like a powerful drug. To feel significant, I needed validation that I was worth being seen, being heard, and confirmation that I was enough. So, like Ipkiss, when I felt invisible, I put on a mask like it was a statement piece to a cute outfit.

The Mask entertained in a way that had everyone's attention. He danced, he played instruments, and he caught the attention of his crush and acted a plumb fool that night in the club. He gained the approval of everyone that night, except the boss and his goons, who was the beautiful singer's boyfriend.

I realize now that we can act all we want, but in reality we look unrecognizable to our Little Girl. She knows what she likes and when we say "yes" to something we are supposed to say "no" to, she is not happy. We may please others, but we are displeasing and even unacceptable to our own selves.

One of *The Mask*'s signature lines was, "Somebody stop me!" I didn't think too much about it over twenty years ago when I first watched the movie. But, that statement resembles the inner self calling out to stop the tug of war that is going on inside. Deep down, I knew who I was presenting myself on life's stage as was not who I really was or wanted to be. I struggled in silence to fight the urges to speak out in fear of being called a rebel. I held back time and again and went along with the program to receive applause and atta-girls. I craved attention and acceptance and my mask was making it happen for me. The truth is that the mask took over my life in the worst of ways. My mask was an entertaining performance for an audience that did not care to see me for me. I hated wearing it, but once again, felt stuck with something that kept me from reaching my true identity.

After all of the mayhem The Mask caused in the movie, Ipkiss realized that The Mask was causing more trouble than good. He tried to throw it away, but it would not let him go. He threw it away and it somehow kept resurfacing. It wasn't until after an array of events that he redeemed himself by helping the police catch the nightclub criminals. He was able to get rid of the mask by throwing the mask as far as he could into the ocean. He threw it away, not because others finally approved of him. No, it was because he finally listened to his truth (aka his gut) that told him he was enough without it. His truth was only confirmed by having the girl of his dreams by his side—his nightclub babe.

**Hey, Little Girl:** Do you remember the first Halloween costume you made when you were thirteen? You cut up old rags and a sheet to make a zombie costume and wore a pillowcase over your head as a mask. You felt silly in a way but knew that the added touches of red marker around the mouth and black smudge marks would add that spooky touch you were going for. That mask was supposed to be worn for that one occasion, but unfortunately it became symbolic to how I lived life every day, never realizing how it would affect us now. Wearing masks was not a treat, but a trick I played on us to gain unconditional love and acceptance. I played the part of the chameleon to fit in and to avoid being alone.

But now, the only part of acting I am interested in is practicing how I am going to show up as the Delabeling Unmasked Me. We are beautiful in appearance and in essence. I learned a valuable lesson while watching you dance. My life's grand performance is for an audience of one … the audience of ME!

**Hey, Dear Reader:** This chapter is written as a caution. Hiding behind a mask does not take us toward our authentic selves, it only hides us from our patterns which need to be processed and healed. It is so easy to go from taking off labels to putting on a mask. As my children and I made masks from paper mache, I could clearly visualize how each layer of newspaper (labels) could evolve into a hardened mask. In the same way, your labels can turn into masks if we use them as a cover-up during this Delabeling Process. Unwanted labels are meant to be scorched to a crisp, not repurposed for a mask.

Like changing your outfit to attend a formal wedding,

you don't want to change out of your gym clothes into sweatpants. It would still be inappropriate attire. Wearing a mask is tacky and inappropriate attire for your life's grand performance.

When we do not know who we are without labels, it's easy to mimic some or take on a full time alter ego. And the longer you wear the mask, the more you will become dependent on it. You will eventually believe it is who you really are. *The Mask* is a clear depiction of that. It can be tempting to forsake your former self and grab hold of a personality we admire. There is nothing wrong with admiration, but oftentimes, it can turn into mimicking someone else's character instead of digging deep to unfold your true essence. *The Mask* is an example of how we can peel off the labels, but still forsake ourselves. *Get Real: The Hazards of Living Out of Your False Self* by Barry Weinhold, helps us understand three descriptions of how substituting a mask for labels may look.

**False Persona** – needed to minimize conflict, rejection, judgement. *"The false self is an artificial persona that people create to protect themselves from re-experiencing developmental trauma, shock, and stress in close relationships."*

**Alter Ego** – needed to gain approval, acceptance, and grandeur. *"The alter ego is another version of oneself who behaves* *similar to yourself yet has recognizable differences in performance that can cause mental instabilities and dangerous consequences."*

**Reinvention** – needed to fit in, belong when feeling like one is not enough. Reinvention is an adjustment to what's trendy or to adopt to a new way of being to gain approval from others—this is my definition for superficial reinvention, not wanting to obtain genuine internal change. There is nothing wrong with the word "reinvention," if it is done so in a transformative way.

One of the reasons false personas, alter egos, and superficial reinventions happen is fear. Your fictional self is who you are when you have a social mask on to please everyone else. As long as we care about what others think of us, we will operate in fear, failing to showcase the multi-facet being that the world is waiting for. The only way to truly conquer this fear is to get to know yourself and present yourself in your purest form. After identifying the labels, unveiling the lies, and embracing the truth, and after forgiving yourself and others, get to know and fall deeply in-love with you.

A false persona, an alter ego, and a superficial reinvention also manifests as a security blanket. Building a "wall" to protect our sore spots from getting touched, hurt, and seen is a natural response. However, just because it is a natural response, does not mean it is a self-nurturing response. When you barricade yourself in to keep people from experiencing the real you, you also keep them from loving the real you. Let's address the elephant in the room… No matter how amazing a person you are, everyone is not for you and will not like you. So hiding yourself to protect yourself is a disadvantage not only for yourself, but for others who need a person like you in their life. You may not be for everybody, but, Dear Friend, you are for somebody! If a butterfly hid itself in a cocoon, it would die. Though butterflies have predators, its focus is not on what can be done to it, but what it can do with its new wings. So, while I truly get the temptation to build a hedge of safety and hiding from the adversaries of your world, there are like-minded people out there ready to meet and embrace the authentic you.

## THE MASKS WE WEAR

Therese J. Borchard, mental health writer and advocate, identified ten mask we wear that keeps us from our authentic selves.

### 1. The Cool Gal

On the outward appearances, this woman seems to have mastered whatever it takes to stay cool, calm, and collected in all situations. However, beneath the surface, one of two things happens. Her bottled-up emotions either result in a nervous breakdown, or she periodically presses the release valve when no one is around, snapping at folks subordinate to her. She lambasts the waiter for forgetting her coffee or fires off a nasty email to her assistant for a small error.

## 2. The Humorist

Humor is a brilliant defense mechanism. I use it myself. If you're laughing, you're not crying, even though they can look the same. That said, it can and does prevent intimacy. Sarcasm, especially, tends to be rooted in pain and is not without consequences.

The humorist tells a joke to skirt sincere discussions, to keep conversations from getting too real or deep. Uncomfortable with conflict, she will charm her way out of confrontation. Her comedy serves as protective shield. As such, she doesn't allow anyone in, and is lonely.

## 3. The Overachiever

Some people unconsciously pursue perfectionism as a defense against annihilation. If everything is done right, then their world can't fall apart. While the accolades and praise associated with being a perfectionist may provide some temporary relief, the perfectionist is always at the mercy of something going wrong, and therefore lives in a constant state of anxiety. Her stubbornness, obsessiveness, and lack of trust build a barrier between her and her loved ones.

## 4. The Martyr

Most of us know a martyr, a person who boasts that she has single-handedly saved the world with her selfless actions. While martyrs can bring families together with compassion, their exaggeration of sacrifices drives loved ones away. The drama with which they do "good" serves as a protective shield from the very people who they are helping. The martyr secures her place in the world by believing her role is critical, all the while making everyone uncomfortable around her.

## 5. The Bully

Every environment in which we work and play is a 5th grade schoolyard with its shares of bullies. Their assertion of control can be subtle, a gentle manipulation to make you see it their way, or can be aggressive, even physical. While bullies appear to be confident in their forceful delivery of opinions and order, they are innately insecure. They want so badly to be respected that they will break the rules of appropriate conduct to get that esteem. Self-doubt drives their hostile behavior; an obsessive need to feel right that comes at the expense of others' rights and feelings.

## 6. The Control Freak

The control freak uses order and power to achieve a sense of security. By making sure everything is in its proper place, she relieves her fear of the unknown, of ambiguity, of uncertainty. A mother hen, the control freak won't let anyone out of her sight, and assumes responsibility for all those around her, even when they don't want to be cared for. She becomes unraveled when anyone deviates from the plan.

### 7. The Self-Basher

Suffering from a chronic case of unworthiness and insecurity, the self-basher projects a negative view of herself to others. Perhaps unconsciously, she believes that she can insulate herself from hurt by hurting herself first. She, then, berates herself and insults herself as a protective measure against any potential zingers coming her way. Self-deprecation becomes a defense mechanism with which she avoids any risk of intimacy.

### 8. The People-Pleaser

The people-pleaser will go to desperate lengths to win the approval of those around her, because her sense of identity is largely based on the assessment of others. Her values often vacillate depending on the input of the day because she looks to outside sources to validate who she is. This mask-type solicits the advice of friends, doctors, experts, co-workers, and mentors because she lacks a strong foundation. Easily influenced by others, decisions are especially difficult for her.

### 9. The Introvert

The timid person or introvert is deathly afraid of failure and rejection. She would much rather feel the pangs of loneliness than risk not being liked. Like the perfectionist, she is so afraid of making a mistake that she refuses to challenge herself. She blushes easily, is embarrassed easily, and doesn't say much for fear of saying the wrong thing.

### 10. The Social Butterfly

Although the life of the party, the social butterfly is innately lonely. She compensates for feelings of insecurity with her gift of gab and small talk. She has many acquaintances but few, if any, real friends. Although her calendar is packed full of social events, her life lacks meaning. She keeps her conversations superficial because deeper dialogues may expose her anxiety or shed her confident persona.

Does any of these mask descriptions resonate with you? They sure did with me. However, with the wisdom of self-awareness, I knew these masks were keeping me from authentic relationships as well as keeping me stuck in the scabs of childhood.

## AUTHENTIC LIVING

When we take on a false persona, alter ego, or reinvention strategy in place of discovering our authentic self, it is obscured because we lose our chance to remember who we are before the labels. It is like being distracted while driving and missing the exit that would guide us home. Wearing a mask causes us to forget our way amongst the countless thoughts related to our false identity. It is better to learn to live authentically.

American theologian Howard Thurman reminds us that:

*There is something in every one of you that waits and listens for the sound of the genuine in yourself. It is the only true guide you will ever have. And if you cannot hear it, you will all of your life spend your days on the ends of strings that somebody else pulls.*

Either we can be guided by our passions and purpose or we can be controlled by our mask. Like a ventriloquist figure, (aka a "ventriloquist dummy") we may look like we are acting on our own accord, but if we are masked, we are being controlled by ideals, opinions, and views that keep us entangled with antiquated labels. We are no dummies, so it's time to throw away the mask!

## WHO AM I WITHOUT THE MASK?

If Ipkiss would have continued the life of The Mask, he would have forfeited so many opportunities that were in his reach. The beautiful club singer fell in love with Ipkiss not The Mask. Someone somewhere in the world needs to hear from you, not your mask! You never know who will appreciate exactly who you are and how you are. Hiding behind masks is hiding from a Little Girl that needs to be inspired by you.

Hide-n-Seek was one of the most memorable games to play as a kid. Imagine that it was your turn to seek, and when you find your friend, she comes out of the hiding place in a scary mask. You would probably scream and run away, right? People are looking for you … the real you! So, there is no better time to throw away those masks you've been hiding behind and step out as your genuine self.

So, who are you without the mask? What are your likes and dislikes? What makes you giddy? What brings peace to your soul? What are your guilty pleasures? What are you passionate about? You may not have had the opportunity to focus on simple questions like these—the smallest characteristics that define your uniqueness matter.

The details that we often overlook may be our superpowers. Have you ever watched a Marvel or Avengers movie and paid attention to their reaction when they realize their specific superpower? When they realize their specific superpowers, they are shocked and enamored by their newfound abilities. In reality, the superpower they are given usually matches their personality already. IF there were no inner spark, then there would be nothing to empower. But, when the spark is ignited, the fire that lies deep within is supernaturally magnified because of some mystical endowment.

You have a spark in you that has the power to light your own world on fire. I love the iconic anthem "This Girl is on Fire" by Alicia Keys. This song reminds me that you have all you need inside of you to set ablaze the past labels that are trying to kill your inner peace and to light the way into your promising future. And you know what else fire can do? Affect everyone around them. Then they will be, "*Smokin'*," too. Now, that's powerful! And you know what else is powerful?! Accepting that YOU ARE THE SHERO OF YOUR STORY, not the mask.

The fact that you are reading this book will help you get unstuck from past labels that do not serve you anymore and make you a Shero. You have accepted the challenge to do the hard work, to dig deep to free your Little Girl … that makes you a Shero. When you are brave enough to be vulnerable with the Little Girl in you, to rescue her from the villains who directly and indirectly tried to destroy her future … that makes you a Shero. The ability to declare to your Little Girl that you are defeating the enemies of her past and slaying the adversaries of her present to conquer and take her rightful place which God has designed for her, makes you the Shero!

Think about the masks you wear and commit to taking them off. You do not need a mask. Hold your gifts out to the world—no apology, no shame, no regrets. As the old saying goes, "Every creature has its rightful place, and in that place it becomes beautiful." All you need is to show up as your authentic-unapologetic-unique-beautiful self that I know you desire to B.E.

## Delabeling Exercise

1. Think about the masks you have held onto.

2. Ask yourself whether the negative message is true?

3. Why am I wearing that mask?

4. If I take it off, what would happen?

5. Enter your answers on the mask below, then use RED ink to draw a big "X" across the mask. "X" marks the spot … you have found the **Limiting Inner Emotions**. Now, **Take Real Understanding To Heart**

## Example

**LIE**: I have to act happy even when I am feeling down so no one around me will feel uncomfortable.

**TRUTH**: I have God-given emotions and will feel them as they come. I will learn and practice Emotional Intelligence to master my emotions.

**LIE**: No one loves me!

**TRUTH**: I know I have people who love me for me. Most importantly, I LOVE ME!

# Your Turn (Grab a journal if needed to list more.)

*Mask Emotion*

LIE:_________________________________

_________________________________

_________________________________

TRUTH: ____________________

_________________________________

_________________________________

*Mask Emotion*

LIE:_________________________________

_________________________________

_________________________________

TRUTH: ____________________

_________________________________

_________________________________

*Mask Emotion*

LIE:_________________________________

_________________________________

_________________________________

TRUTH: ____________________

_________________________________

_________________________________

# CHAPTER 6: JUST B.E. (BECOME AND EVOLVE)

## (Step Five of the Delabeling Process)

*"To be or not to be ... that is the question..."*

-WILLIAM SHAKESPEARE

WILLIAM SHAKESPEARE'S FAMOUS LINE IN *The Tragedie of Hamlet* drama was a timeless one that I have asked myself since starting my Delabeling Process. Essentially, the quote proposed a thought provoking question asking if it is better to live or better to die. This prolific poet was referring to a decision between this life and the afterlife. When I think of the word "BE," dying isn't the real tragedy. To me, the real tragedy would be dying without the opportunity to B.E. (**B**ecome and **E**volve).

Michelle Obama shared her extraordinary and inspiring story in her memoir, *Becoming*. One of the main themes this book accentuated was PROCESS. Reading about her childhood, how she was accepted into prestigous schools and colleges, the loss of her father, her career moves, how she met and married her husband, how she managed her family, and all the strain and opposition she experienced, I realized that she did not magically arrive at her pinnacle moments, she had to go through many processes, which led her to becoming the First Lady of the United States of America. The process is not always easy, but it is well worth it. The Empty Chair Process was intimidating, but in order for my Little Girl to get unstuck, I needed to start and trust the process. I did not know it then, but pouring out my heart to my younger self, in a way I have never done before, gave strength to my Little Girl to move from the place she'd been for far too long. She stood ready for her marching orders. But, the sad thing was, I did not know what direction to lead her in.

## WHO HAVE I BECOME?

I know what it was like to be stuck in a stupor, but who is this person taking a stand? When I think of the word "become," I define it as coming from an old position into an unknown and uncomfortable position of being. To become is to enter into a new space that can feel uniquely different than the space you were once in. To become is more of a physical change. For example, when some people gain or lose weight, their physical appearance not only looks different, but they become a whole new dress size as well. To evolve, however, is to experience a mental transformation. Using the same above example, if she has evolved, her communication about herself and others will be completely different because of a mental upgrade.

One of the important lessons that grabbed hold of me from the book *Becoming* was Michelle Obama's bravery to travel multiple school buses to a new school outside of her district to obtain a great education. She was a young girl traveling all that way, never mentioning being afraid or lonely on her venture. Unfortunately, I could never see myself voluntarily traveling too far from my family. That "lonely" label limited me from finding true passion and joy outside of my circle of family and church friends. I worked hard through my years to fit in where I could with people I knew from childhood, surely it would be ten times as hard to do so with people I did not know.

For someone who represents herself as independent, my label caused me to be dependent on others to help me feel a sense of belonging. Even so, in the midst of people, I would still feel lonely like I was somewhere in the middle of nowhere.

## IT FINALLY CLICKED FOR ME.

A few years ago, on a Sunday morning, I had the feeling of loneliness overtaking me. Even in a room full of people, somehow that childhood label crept its way into my energetic space and made me feel like I did not belong anywhere or to anyone. The church was full of people, and everyone was greeting one another and engaging in small talk, I heard laughter in one ear and music and whispers in the other. But, still, there was a disconnection and so much space between everyone in that building and myself.

I caught the eye of a dear friend and confidant whom I affectionately call Mom D. She was old enough to be my mother, but we had a deep connection and bond that sealed a genuine friendship. I could tell Mom D sensed something bothering me. She has some type of bionic super vision that could see right through me. I could be laughing and socializing with others, but somehow she could see behind the mask and into my lonely soul. She asked me to sit with her for a few minutes to "chat," but I could feel that this conversation was about to be like a soul reading. As soon as she asked, *"So, what's up with you?"* my eyes watered. I was able to articulate exactly how I felt putting words together in the strangest way... *"I feel stuck, like I am somewhere in the middle of nowhere."* She looked at me and smiled warmly, *"I get that."* Then she said something that changed my perception of loneliness forever.

> *"Sometimes God has you in a place, where you will feel*
> *lonely, but it is really Him setting you apart."*

I sat there and stared at her like I saw her for the very first time. It was as if her words seeped into the empty filling in those spaces of my soul. I cannot remember how long I sat quietly or what she said after that, but I do remember tears flowing down my face as if I had found the keys to set the caged bird inside of me free. The words she shared that day aligned with the truth that was deep down inside all along. "*I am not alone, I am set apart…*" That phrase was on repeat in my head and still is today.

Now, don't get me wrong, the idea of being set apart took some getting used to, because set apart still meant separated from other people on many levels. Eventually, I realized that I did not need other people to become, I only needed myself… I was enough! Just like seeds that are sorted by a gardener, I understood that God was not trying to bury me, He was planting me so I would be rooted in purpose that would evolve into something beautiful and fruitful. I always felt different and out of place, but overtime I realized that being alone or set apart was no longer a bad thing. It was a destiny thing.

**Hey, Little Girl**: There is a vast difference between loneliness, aloneness, and being set part. Loneliness is when you do not have connection with the community of family or friends. Aloneness is a disconnection from your core identity. I know you have suffered from both forms of connections on a physical and spiritual level. When I affirmed you during our therapy session, you defined what it is to BECOME by getting up from a stuck place and entering into a new phase of being. But then, when you affirmed me and gave the gift of forgiveness, you EVOLVED from past labels into a worthy belief system. It took me a while to fully understand, but when you chose to just B.E., you supernaturally transferred that into your present self.

So, that brings me to another exciting thought! If you were able to emanate such a power energy that helped me evolve into a better me, then I, too, have the wherewithal to radiate my future self into manifesting the best version of me!

**Hey, Dear Reader:** From the time a caterpillar is laid on a leaf as an egg, it instinctively knows that the sole function in life is to eat. This is the way of being for a caterpillar—going from dill weeds to milkweed to cabbage eating as much as possible from larvae until it reaches adulthood. After becoming an adult, the caterpillar enters a new stage where it sheds its skin to form another skin called a chrysalis. What once crawled around eating all day, was now stationed and still in a new form of being. After about nine to fourteen days, the caterpillar comes out of the chrysalis presenting itself much differently than before … now it has wings! The stages of how a caterpillar becomes a butterfly is always a fascinating process. The real mind-blowing stage for me, however, is the time it takes to emerge from the place after it sheds its chrysalis to the time it actually flies. It takes a few hours for the blood to travel through the veins of the wings to expand so it will be strong enough to fly. The butterfly is already in its new physical form, but it still takes time for it to evolve into what it has become.

To BECOME is a physical transformation. To EVOLVE is a mentality transformation. I have a big imagination, so I am thinking that as the butterfly is sitting on the tree, it is trying to come to grips with what in the world has happened. *"I know how to crawl on my belly at a steady pace ensuring that I camouflage so I will not be eaten by predators. I know what to eat, when to eat, and where to eat. But I don't know how to fly!"*

These are the same caterpillar thoughts we have sometimes. We know how to operate as we always have. We know how to fit in, when to laugh, when to agree, and when to avoid opposition by people pleasing or evading. But, throughout this Delabeling Process, something has changed in us. We have become unstuck and are changing positions from victim to victor. We are no longer poor in spirit; we have become mentally and emotionally powerful. We are no longer concerned about others' opinions of us; we have become confident and omnipotent in the realm of knowing who we represent now.

Like the blood flows through the wings of a butterfly, so does the warm energetic F.L.U.I.D flow through you. F.L.U.I.D is a mnemonic that stands for...

***Forward-thinking*** – the ability to push through a difficult place with emotional intelligence and empathy.

***Luminous*** – an inner bright light that can no longer be contained by the darkness of self-doubt and unworthiness.

***Uniqueness*** – standing alone in ability, creativity, essence, energy, spirit, and thought with pride.

***Identity*** – distinguished, yet recognizable for what one represents, supports, and believes.

***Destiny*** – a rightful place reserved for the near future.

When you are ready to fly, F.L.U.I.D strengthens your wings, readying you to soar past labels that have been keeping you from your purpose.

When the butterfly's wings are fully expanded, reaching two times the size of his thorax, it is strong enough to soar to heights it has never been before. Once a caterpillar is metamorphosed into a butterfly, even if it lands on the ground, it cannot do the same thing it once did. When you become and evolve, it is impossible for you to return to the same thought processes, react to things the same way, or accept old viewpoints as your truth.

Dr. Benjamin Hardy, an organizational psychologist, offers seven ways to know you have evolved:

1. **You feel like you're where you're supposed to be...** As an evolved person, you feel a higher sense of purpose in your life, like you've been guided. You are in the right place and on the right path. This is more than a mere belief—but a spiritual confirmation. You are aligned with your highest self and manifesting the life you were meant to live.

2. **Your life is simpler...** As an evolved person, you have simplified your life. There is an art in slowing down and smelling the flowers. You're not racing through life. You're present. You prefer experiences over stuff. You've removed everything from your life that distracts you from your highest purpose. Everything in your life makes sense being there. It's purposeful.

3. **You attract the right people into your life...** As an evolved person, you attract the right people into your life. You are moving toward a huge vision and the needed connections and mentors always seem to show up right when

you need them. "When the student is ready the teacher will appear."

4. **You feel a gap between yourself and those you used to associate with...** As an evolved person, you feel a gaping chasm between yourself and the people you used to spend time with. This is perhaps one of the saddest parts of becoming evolved, and one of the hardest. At some point in every evolved person's journey, they have to disband themselves from people who pull them down. However, once they did, it wasn't long before they were nothing like their old friends.

5. **You notice the truth hidden in every-thing...** As an evolved person, you notice subtle truth and connections in everything, while watching movies, having conversations, and driving in your car. Life is your teacher. You are deeply connected to the universe and are sensitive to even the smallest connections and lessons.

6. **You care more about other people—but less about what they think of you...** As an evolved person, you care intensely about other people's wellbeing. However, you no longer care what other people think about you. Other people's perceptions no longer govern you. As Martha Graham has said, "What people in the world think of you is really none of your

business."

7. **You genuinely want the best for others…**
   As an evolved person, you are happy when other people succeed and sad when other people fail. The success of others is seen as the success of the whole. You genuinely want what's best for everyone—even those you would consider your enemies. You only have love for every person on earth. No hatred, envy, or guile.

An evolved woman illuminates a fluorescent light that projects her new identity so much so that no one can deny the F.L.U.I.D circulating through her veins rendering her new life. This prodigious process of becoming and evolving is so well worth it if you are ready to fly. Just be open to experiencing life through whole new lenses. Your new perspective on life will bring happiness, creativity, and productiveness in ways you have never experienced before. A Delabeled woman has a growing consciousness of her inner ability to glide through life remembering the lessons of her past but trusting the process that is leading her into the place she is meant to B.E!

<hr>

## Delabeling Exercise

---

Shakespeare had an inner battle to be, but we know what we want: WE WANT TO LIVE AND SOAR!

**Reflection:** Review Dr. Hardy's evidence of evolving on pages 10-13. Use this list to reflect on how far you have come and where you have evolved to thus far.

Forward-thinking: Because you will never stop the process to B.E., journal three or more ways you would like to become and evolve.

# CHAPTER 7: FOCUS ON YOURSELF

**(Step Seven: Delabeling Process)**

*"You lose a lot of people when you focus on yourself. Find no shame in evolving."*

-Billy Chapata

"the gift of helps"...that was the results of a ministry survey I took to find where I would be most impactful at my former church. I wasn't surprised by the results, helping was my thing.

At a very young age, I enjoyed helping my mom sort and wash clothes. I loved the fresh clean scent, handing my mom the clothes to be hung up on the clothesline and then running through the clothes enjoying the breeze and the cool touch of garments that grazed my skin. When I was older, my mom depended on me to help out with my younger siblings and even keep an eye on things while she ran errands. My intention was always to take some of the stress from a woman I saw trying her hardest to maintain a household, work, take night classes at a local college, and keep a roof over our heads. I was nicknamed "Momma Nia" because I acted like a mini mom with helping around the house. I was nicknamed "Peace Maker" by my friends because I helped resolve quarrels and fights. I was nicknamed "Church Girl" by my classmates because I helped with classwork and advised them on how to stay out of trouble … helping in school and wearing long skirts everyday equated to a good girl in their eyes. I knew how to help others. When it came to myself, however, I did not know how to help myself fulfill the dreams I longed for.

I wanted to be an African dancer ever since I saw the movie *Coming to America*. The polyrhythmic movements and music were so captivating and the sporadic yells and the synchronized sounds as they danced was communicating freedom and passion I was attracted to. After that, I wanted to be a flight attendant, not so I could travel the world, but because I always wished I existed as a bird soaring the clear blue skies congregating on the highest cloud with my bird-ie friends. As a teenager, I wanted to be a businesswoman in any career where I would wear black, silky pantyhose (don't laugh too hard). My sisters and I wore knee highs until we were old enough to wear stockings, but could only afford the ones from the hair store that cost a dollar and would cause a run as soon as you walked too fast in them. I promised myself that when I was old enough, I would wear the "real" $5.49 stockings that come in the little box.

These were silly career dreams, but these were *my silly career dreams*. As I matured, I was unclear about my career path. I found myself distracted by the conditions of my family and always trying to figure out how I could help. There seemed to be no time to focus on any dreams, silly or not, because I was always helping others with their dreams.

I HAD A DREAM, BUT I HAD A DECISION TO MAKE... I could attend college right out of high school, or I could get a job and help my mom financially. I chose to help my mom. I HAD ANOTHER DECISION TO MAKE... I could attend college after I got married, or we could use the money to pay our utilities and groceries (we were married young and the struggle was real). We chose to pay the bills. THEN, THERE WAS ANOTHER DECISION... I could work to pay for daycare and school, or I could be a stay-at-home mom. I chose to be a stay-at-home mom. I CAN NOT FORGET ABOUT THIS DECISION… I could step away from all of my ministry responsibilities for a season and finish my degree or continue to help my church function and "whatsoever your hands find to do" do that to help advance the ministry. I chose to help my church.

All of these choices were great ones. Somehow, in the midst of me making great choices for everyone else, I wasn't choosing myself. Could I have done both? Sure, I could have. So, what was holding me back? The same recurring feelings that paralyze Little Girls of all colors, race, and creed … guilt and shame.

"Don't be selfish!" I was taught at an early age in my home. In a house of eight children, we had to share toys, pass down clothes, and share space. My parents did not want us to grow up thoughtless and inconsiderate of others, but at the same time the consistent teachings to be considerate of others taught us how to never prioritize ourselves. This lesson was doubled down when we went to church. Many young people went from graduating high school to getting a job to help out their families or started families of their own. I had a hard time with this notion because I desired to attend college right out of high school.

I remember hearing a preacher suggest: "If you can't find your passion in the church, then maybe it is not God leading you to that passion." If dreams reached outside of the church's four walls were deemed a sin… I never got a chance to read about passions being a sin in the bible, but I believed what was ingrained in me over the pulpit and at family bible classes. I was the kind of child that wanted to get it right with my parents, other adults, and God the first time. So, I held on to every word from the adults in my life and tried to obey the spoken and suggested rules that were implemented.

So, my dream to graduate from college to fulfil any one of my "silly" dreams became a fleeting thought. The conviction of dreaming big piled so high that I could not see over the mountain of guilt and shame for wanting to prioritize myself. I resisted being selfish, but inadvertently became attached to "selflessness"… another label that caused me to think less of myself and more of others. I do not blame my family or church, wholeheartedly, for my labels. At an impressionable age, how I internalized the past messages influenced my thought process and behavior in adulthood. From those teachings, there have been subtle triggers and beliefs I've battled that kept me limited.

My selflessness label influenced most of my decisions causing me to suppress my dreams to go to college. Even still, there was a nagging nudge to further my education. As I think back on my life choices, another leading factor for choosing to help instead of pursuing my dreams was my addiction to being wanted and needed. The gratefulness, thankfulness, and praise from the people equated to being seen and wanted in my eyes, but I would soon learn how out of focus that thought process was. I was absorbed in the idea of belonging and feeling significant, instead of attentive to my dreams. There was a tug-of-war going on … others versus my dreams. The battle was mentally and emotionally exhausting.

Trying to be everything to everyone is just unwise. I needed to get real with myself. The reality is, **I cannot focus on everything!** If I did not steady my Android phone to capture a picture of my son in the midst of his friends as he received his "all-star" award at his school ceremony, the image would have focused on every student and everything around him or the image would've been blurry and unusable. Once I tapped my screen on my son, the camera focused and captured a clear picture of him with everything complimenting him in the background (I've since gotten an iPhone and the camera focuses instantly. But this is not a battle of cell phone providers so don't @ me!) (LOL).

In the same way, in order to focus on myself, I needed to tap into what I wanted to capture for my life for once. This was a real struggle in my mid-thirties. I did not realize at the time there was a cost to helping others. While I was seeking to be appreciated by helping others, my life's goals and dreams were depreciating. I was accustomed to showing up for others, but rarely showed up for myself in the way I needed to so my dreams would come to fruition.

In order for me to B.E., I first had to learn how to focus on myself … the operative word being learn. When I gave myself the permission to zero in on what was pulling me toward more, I realized that obtaining my degree was not only an outward reward anymore, but an inward push toward my life's purpose. My middle name means "advisor," so counseling seemed to be destined from a child. It was an innate gift I was ready to give and I knew obtaining my degree would provide the education I needed to become a mental health counselor and provide adequate services to the youth and their families to help them thrive as a family unit.

So, while my gift of help was indeed a gift, it needed to be focused on to fulfil my dreams and life purpose instead of others. Of all the choices I made, giving up on my dreams was NEVER A CHOICE. I just needed to learn how to focus!

**Hey, Little Girl:** You were always a bridesmaid and never a bride.

You thought the noble thing to do was to promote others instead of yourself. I have learned that the gift of helping is a wonderful characteristic, but it can also be a hindrance to yourself and others. You are worthy of your silly dreams, your innate passions, and your God-given purpose. I choose to focus on us now. This type of focus brings clarity in ways people may not understand but will have no choice but to respect.

**Hey, Dear Reader:** Be careful not to focus on just helping people. In our quest to help others, we have to ensure we are not hindering. Instead, focus on your goals that will in turn help people. As the saying goes, "Give a man a fish, feed him for a day; teach a man how to fish, feed him for a lifetime."

For example, if you are a Time Management Consultant, you would not help your client by watching their kids, cleaning their house, picking up their clothes from the dry cleaners, and doing their budget. *(Director's Cut: Another thing this does, by the way, is that it not only does not serve your purpose but paralyzes your client from B.E.)* Your goal would be to teach your client how to prioritize daily tasks, minimize inefficiency, and reduce distractions to cultivate better habits and develop a productive lifestyle. When you focus on your goals, you will be able to help a lot of people while fulfilling your passions. Teaching someone how to be self-sufficient is different than trying to take on the responsibilities of a person.

Helping people to help themselves is productivity for both parties. Our goal as helpers, is not to randomly take on others' responsibilities, but to help by telling others how to better take care of themselves. Showing others how to find resources, teaching someone how to work a computer, or how to become financially stable is time well spent where the learner will flourish on their own and you will fulfill your goals, too.

Sacrificing dreams by taking on other people's responsibilities and injecting yourself in various situations to be a help is not noble. On the contrary, when you are overly helpful, you are taking away the opportunity for the person you are trying to help to learn how to do for themselves. Now, there is a risk of developing an unhealthy relationship that can cause codependence.

In its simplest terms, a codependent relationship is when one partner needs the other partner, who in turn, needs to be needed. This circular relationship is the basis of what experts refer to when they describe the "cycle" of codependency. In these types of relationships, the code-pendent person feels worthless unless they are needed by the enabler and making drastic sacrifices for the enabler. While the enabler gets satisfaction from getting their every need met, the inner struggle to focus on one's own dreams brings on extreme conflict because self-identity is centered on sacrificing goals to be a helper. It becomes next to im-possible for the co-dependent to check in on herself, so she stays super focused on how others feel.

**The best way to stop the dysfunctional relation-ship of co-dependency is to break the cycle and become selfish.** Choose to focus on yourself. This will not make sense to many people, especially an enabler. Like me, I am sure you were taught that selfishness was a bad word and an even worse behavior. But what if we think of selfishness in a different light? I like to think of selfishness as one fishing for self. You see the suffix "ness" is added to an adjective to make the word a noun. So, the positive twist to "selfishness" would be the quality of searching and seeking for self.

I went on a fishing trip with a group and my father-in-law taught us the functions of different fishing poles, the best bait for a particular fish, and how to throw the line out without getting it tangled. Among all that we learned while preparing to be great fishermen and women, the most important lesson taught was patience.

The takeaway from the fishing trip helped me look at selfishness in a different light. In the quest of helping yourself focus on your dreams, there has to be a line thrown out into the deep parts. Your hook and reel in are what you need to focus on to help you on this Delabeling Journey. Here are "Seven Self Catches" you can fish for every day:

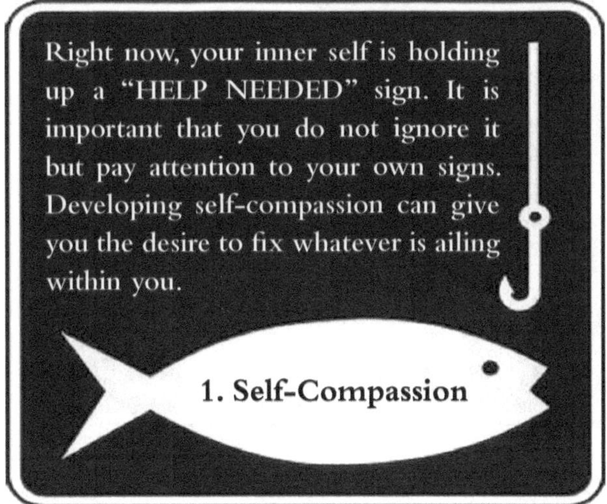

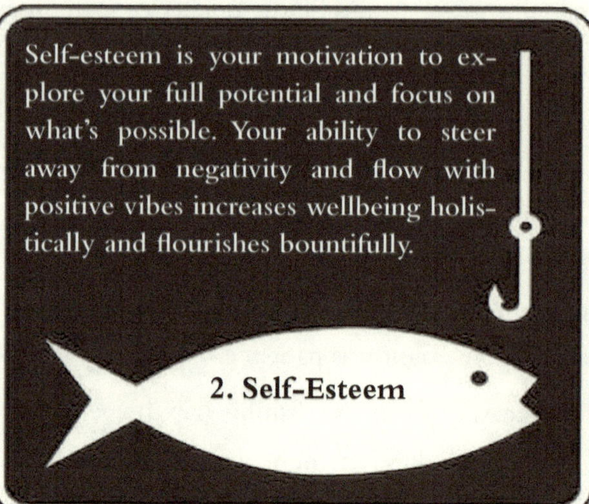
Self-esteem is your motivation to explore your full potential and focus on what's possible. Your ability to steer away from negativity and flow with positive vibes increases wellbeing holistically and flourishes bountifully.
2. Self-Esteem

Love yourself enough to stop the negative talk and start celebrating your milestones. Embrace how valuable you are and recognize that the more you love yourself, the less nonsense you will tolerate, and the more inner peace you will generate.
3. Self-Love

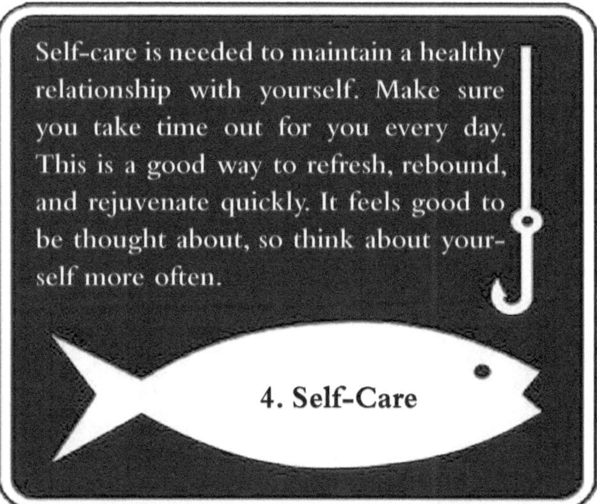
Self-care is needed to maintain a healthy relationship with yourself. Make sure you take time out for you every day. This is a good way to refresh, rebound, and rejuvenate quickly. It feels good to be thought about, so think about yourself more often.
4. Self-Care

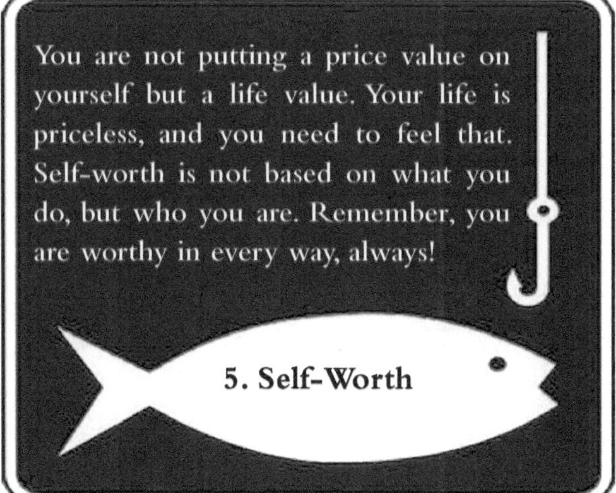
You are not putting a price value on yourself but a life value. Your life is priceless, and you need to feel that. Self-worth is not based on what you do, but who you are. Remember, you are worthy in every way, always!
5. Self-Worth

As a good manager, you manage your time well, achieve goals, and organize your life. Powerful and strong-minded women are ones who don't have it all together but are intentional about developing skills to succeed and carry out their dreams.

**6. Self-Management**

Teach others how to respect you by respecting yourself. The friends you have, the places you go, and the things you do are all signs of your respect levels. Self-respect is the foundation of dignity and the "how-to" guide in relationships.

**7. Self-Respect**

**"To move on quickly, find someone else. To move on truly, find yourself!"** After removing past labels and throwing away the mask, taking time to get to know yourself is the healthiest thing to do. This in no way equates to becoming egotistical or a narcissist. Contrarily, what you reel in from self-fishing are all integrated with one another to enhance mental, emotional, and physical, spiritual, and social health. More importantly, good selfishness is a sign of empathy.

When you empathize with yourself, you suspend all judgement, you are self-accepting, and you recognize that past labels are a part of your story. The focus is solely on how you can heal, learn, and grow closer to the best parts of you. It's not about leaving others out, but all about bringing self-awareness in. It's about realizing that you are calling forth your desires and needs in life. Focusing on yourself is about celebrating every intriguing part of you because as Melissa Fredericks, author of Journey of Self Love exclaims, "You are worth it... As is. Without change. Without exception!"

Delabeling Exercise

---

### Let's Go Fishing!

Cast your lines and think about what you want to pull from deep within yourself. How can you focus on yourself a little more to reach goals or to move closer to fulfilling a dream—yes, even those silly dreams? Be patient with yourself if nothing comes to mind right away. As soon as you hook that thought, write it down along with a plan to reel in the things you are worthy of.

Have fun with it! Are you ready?

Go Fish!

# Part III: THE LIBERATED GIRL

# CHAPTER 8: YOUR FLEET OF S.H.I.Ps

## (Step Nine of the Delabeling Process)

*"Community means strength that joins our strength to do the work that needs to be done. Arms to hold us when we falter. A circle of healing. A circle of friends. Someplace where we can be free."*

– Starhawk

What happens when a Warrior Woman has a fleet of S.H.I.Ps?

Queen of Dragons Daenerys Targaryen (Khaleesi), from *Game of Thrones*, was a warrior woman determined to take her rightful place as queen.

In her early teens she was exiled from her home and traded in marriage by her abusive older brother for an army to help him reclaim their father's throne. When her brother lost control and was murdered, her character emerged strong, confident, and courageous. She then had the boldness to make plans to reclaim the Iron Throne, seeing it as her birthright. Several obstacles delayed her process of recapturing her kingdom, but her determination and ruthless fight against slave owners made her a relentless leader. She was able to form an army of freed people and secured a reliable fleet of ships that ultimately helped her win the war against her adversaries. As she fought for her dreams to take back her family's throne, her fight became her fleet's fight. She now had an allegiance with powerful people to help her claim her place as Targaryen Queen.

Khaleesi's character in *Game of Thrones* was one of the most profound descriptions of how an army and a fleet of ships backing you can make you a queen even before you get to the throne. Back in that day, the more ships a leader had the stronger they appeared to be. Even though Khaleesi had a strong moral compass and a tenacity to help others along the way, that alone was not enough. She needed a strong backing to push her to her rightful place. Each ship had its purpose, and each ship had the capacity to protect Khaleesi in their own way.

The purpose of a fleet is to have a group of ships that can work together in battle. These ships are usually a diverse collection of ships of differing capabilities, which include ships to protect the carriers, ships to supply food, fuel and material to the carriers, ships with extra personnel that provide services and replacements in times of war.

In a larger fleet, like the U.S. Navy, fleets are responsible for carrying air crafts, protecting borders, controlling the waters, watching for intruders, blocking enemy submarines, and carrying Marine personnel. A fleet of ships are essential to any captain during a voyage. In *Game of Thrones*, Khaleesi's fleet helped give her the prestige and power to not only take back her father's throne, but to ultimately become queen over the Northern part of the world.

Watching how Khaleesi formed a fleet to reach her dynasty reminded me of how grateful I am for my fleet for helping me during my Delabeling Process. When I decided to not allow the labels of my past to be the compass on my life's journey, I knew I would need help rebuilding. It would take some renovations to improve broken thought processes, refurbish outdated habits, and remove damaged relationships to create more space for inspiring ones. In order to cultivate a powerful life, I needed a powerful fleet. Like Khaleesi, there was a mission inside of me to build a trusted fleet of ships to revive and strengthen me to be and achieve the best in life. It took time to build my fleet, not because of skepticism, but rare jewels are hard to find. Developing genuine relationships with like-minded people is like finding treasure.

Please allow me to brag on my jewels for a moment. It is priceless to have found friends who reciprocate unconditional love and acceptance. My friends are not perfect, but they are perfect for me. They are supportive through the great and not-so-great times. Learning from past experiences, I worked on being a great friend so I would attract great friends. I learned to make sure my friends know they are loved and adored for being their authentic selves. We encourage one another and challenge one another to B.E. They probably think I'm crazy because every time I see them, especially in person, I yell a "Heyyyyy!" in a high pitch voice with the cheesiest smile followed by the biggest hug I can give. I am grateful and happy every time I get to be in their presence, and I make sure they know it! My friends are my family. They are one of my greatest gifts in this lifetime.

As much as I love my friends, the friend-ship has its capacity. I remembered this lesson during my first year of marriage. I moved to New Jersey away from my family and friends. My husband was my new family, best friend, counselor, partner, and all. One day, he told me I needed other outlets. My feelings were hurt at first, but what he said made sense later. In a house there are many electrical outlets, because one outlet does not have the capacity to be the power source for everything you want to plug in. A functional home would need electrical outlets in every room so various items with a plug can reach. In the same way, my husband could not be my end all be all. I needed people around me that had the capacity and wherewithal to help me plug into different sectors of life. It can be overwhelming for one person to be your all-in-all, but when you have a fleet, you have carriers with unique abilities to travel with you on your quest.

**Hey, Little Girl:** When it was your time to speak to me in the therapy session, you looked at me, then glanced behind me and then smiled. I remember you saying, *"Wow, look at you! You are so beautiful. I really like your husband; he is nice. And your daughter, she looks like me! I am glad you have great friends who treat you kindly. You have so much fun with them. I didn't want to bother you, but I needed you. I wanted to be with you. I am so proud of you! I am proud of all the lessons you have learned and never stopped trying. I am glad you didn't give up when you felt really sad that time … I am glad we are still here."*

I get why you were looking behind me. You saw something I didn't see at the time. You saw my fleet of ships. You smiled knowing that we would not be here today if there was not a decision to focus on how to cultivate a community that would strengthen us to become greater. You saw what was pushing me forward and the ships that were to come and make my journey a sustainable one. You saw the capacity of each ship and their ability to help reach our destination and take back all the peace, joy, and self-worth that was stolen from us in the form of labels.

You remembered the time when I wanted to give up on life. I am so glad I didn't. I now understand the value in the journey; it is where the magic happens and makes reaching the end goal so sweet. Our fleet is only growing, Little Girl, which is making me stronger and more determined to keep going and never give up. I am glad you can rest in a community that is thriving. I am glad that we have a fleet of S.H.I.Ps.

**Hey, Dear Reader:** Now, that you have chosen to focus on yourself in the most fervent way, you are ready to choose who you will journey your life with. Oh, yes, you have the wherewithal to surround yourself with people who will push you to the next level in life. This crew are people who will be a part of your **Fleet of S.H.I.Ps**. You may or may not be a part of a fleet already. Either way, it is vital to understand the role of every ship and how they will help you claim your rightful place.

When a Warrior Woman has a fleet of **S.H.I.Ps** it **S**trengthens **H**er **I**nner **P**urposes! Each ship has a meaningful impact on her life's voyage. She leads by sailing with ownership of who she is and the power to become and evolve into someone greater. Her accompanying fleet represents healthy bonds in the form of Kinships

(Family), Friendships (Confidants), Companionships (Spouse), Mentorships (Therapist and Coaches), Fellowships (Networks), Championships (Peer Circles), and most importantly Worship (God/Higher Power)! You may not have all of these ships, but here is a brief explanation of ships, in no specific order of importance, that would make a powerful fleet.

**Ownership:** Self-ownership is belonging to yourself first. Brené Brown explains, "True belonging doesn't require you to change who you are, it allows you to be who you are." When you are a part of a fleet, you have to embrace your own sense of self, which involves your ideas, thoughts, skills, and knowledge. Owning your identity, is a sure way to focus on where you are going and how you need your fleet to help you get there.

**Guardianship:** Boundaries are protectors of your energy and space. A guardian assertively sets boundaries to keep out intruders who will make you doubt yourself and unwanted negativity that preys upon your self-esteem and self-confidence.

**Kinship:** "Family is everything" … sometimes. If you have a close knit family, you are among the richest people in the world. If you happen to be in a family that is not close or if someone close to you has passed, then you are still blessed with the ability to formulate your own family with people who I refer to as my spiritual family. The Kinship works together in harmony to ensure that love and guidance is always on board.

**Friendship:** Friendships in the form of confidants are invaluable. A confidant gives sound advice out of love and concern for your well-being. This ship reassures you that no matter what, you have a backbone that will stick with you and by you through any of life's battles.

**Companionship:** This ship is the companionship of a spouse or partner. A healthy companionship makes sure you are always seen, heard, and valued. Your companion supports your vision and dream and is excited about your journey. The love from the union lets you know you are not alone. In the company of ships, your companionship should always make you feel safe, motivated, and reassured that they are sailing with a common goal until the end.

**Mentorship:** This includes Coaches, Counselors, Consultants, and Mentors. Each of these professions has a different job but are on the same ship with the common goal to point you in the right direction. They have the ability to draw a map to your port of call. They also help you regulate psychological and emotional health on your voyage to a greater you.

**Fellowship:** Good fellowship is the cement of a community of ships. Socializing and networking is the part of the fellowship that helps you get organized, create a plan, and solve problems during your quest to access what is possible for you through the connections of others.

**Citizenship:**   Even when finding a community where you belong, insecurity, anxiety, and imposter syndrome may try to creep in. Nevertheless, your clairvoyance accelerates beyond your emotions and reminds you that your purpose is bigger than any fear that tries to steer you. Do not push fear overboard. Take it on the ride and let it become so dumbfounded by its lack of control that it turns into fortitude with no other decision but to keep going!

**Worship:** There are two types of Wor-ships that are advantageous to have in your fleet.

1.  The old English definition for worship derives from worth-ship or worthiness. Always remember you are worthy of a great tribe that supports you, uplifts you, pushes you, thinks the world of you, and loves you! You are worth it!

2.  Whether you reverence God, a High Power, or the Universe, worship is a way to exercise thankfulness. Along your journey, always remember to rest in gratefulness when you reflect on how far you have come and how far you are going. If you cannot find the words to express all the joy you feel within, at any time, just whisper, *"Thank you."*

**Championship:** Your Champion-ship is comprised of physical trainer(s) and cheerleaders. The physical trainer helps you make healthy food choices and gives you exercise regimens to build your physical strength. Cheerleaders can be a part of your training team or they may be training with you. They are your encouragers, supporters, and continuous reminders to stay the course and achieve your physical goals. A powerful championship helps you overcome obstacles and pushes you through the blood, sweat, and tears even when adversity strikes. Having a championship as a part of your fleet means you are already winning, so keep sailing to your victory!

## YOUR FLEET GIVES YOU STRENGTH.

On this voyage, you, too, will need to secure a fleet that will be instrumental in reaching your goals. The journey toward Delabeling is no easy task. It takes a made-up mind to pursue healing and because we are human and have normal emotions, we are going to falter in our feelings to win. Your fleet will not let you lose! Even if you run into the tallest mountain, your fleet will push you over it.

When surrounded by your fleet, it gives you the confidence to battle and capture any mental, emotional, or spiritual enemies on your journey to victory! You are the captain of your ship!

As a captain, you inevitably want to strengthen those who are around you. Just like the proverb, "Iron sharpens iron," the importance of a community is that there is mutual benefit in the rubbing of iron blades together, so the edges become sharper, making the knives more efficient in their task to cut away negative influences and improve their quality of life.

## BEWARE OF TRAUMA RESPONSES.

Without a strong fleet, you may be tempted to stay docked instead of taking a real chance at life. Have you ever heard someone say, "I am a loner" , "I do not need anyone," or "I am good all by myself"? I don't know how many times I said these statements. Going at life alone is not a true desire. It is more than likely a trauma response.

Life Coach Jamila White highlights ultra-independency as conditioning that we submit to as a survival tactic. We would rather shield ourselves from being disappointed or rejected or rather go at life alone instead of being reinjured again. This may seem like a safer choice, but let's face it, we need one another. We need a strong fleet that will cultivate strength in us. A fleet sees in ways you may not see yourself. Just ask three people in your circle how they view you? I bet they highlight some things you did not know they were thinking. A fleet gives you the strength to look deeper within and try again. So, surround yourself with people who are just as excited about your dream as you are.

Sometimes the waves start raging and the journey is scary. But when you have a strong fleet with you, courage and stamina help you ride the waves of life.

## A FLEET CAN HELP YOU REACH YOUR PURPOSE!

Having a fleet broadens your vision and makes dreams into a reality. My book Doula, Coach Geo Derice, is the part of my fleet who encouraged me to write this book. I was pregnant with the possibility of sharing my story with women to help peel off past labels and elevate them into their truest identity. Coach Geo guided me through his First Book Done course, motivating me to push past the pain of doubt and fear, so I would deliver a baby that you now hold in your hands. It's beautiful right?! (Smile)

That is how a fleet of S.H.I.Ps work. It is invaluable when you form relationships with other warriors to help you win! Even when there are times you have to depend solely on ownership for a season, your fleet is always standing by to rally you forward and upward to take your rightful place in the world!

## BONUS TIPS FOR YOUR FLEET OF S.H.I.Ps:

1. **Be open to new opportunities...** The new you will attract new opportunities and they always seem to come when you least expect it, so get ready!

2. **Be open to new friendships...** Making new

friendships in adulthood can be a daunting task, but it is not an impossible one. Most of my FRIENDSHIPs are from meeting beautiful people who love living life to its fullest just like I do. Put yourself out there. Someone needs the friend in you!

3. **Be open to new adventures...** Life is an adventure! Try something you haven't tried before. Go somewhere you have always dreamed of going. You never know what crew member you will meet to make your fleet stronger and complete!

## Delabeling Exercise

*Knowing what part people play in your life is very important on your voyage. Use your journal to answer these questions and get intentional about your fleet of S.H.I.Ps.*

1. What S.H.I.Ps do you have in your fleet?
2. What S.H.I.Ps would you like to recruit to make your fleet stronger?
3. How does your fleet of S.H.I.Ps help you on your quest in life?

# CHAPTER 9: REINTRODUCTION PROCESS

**(Step Nine of the Delabeling Process)**

*"If the person is doing the work of transforming their life and vibrating higher daily (from where they used to be), you no longer know them. Throw away all of your automated responses, assumptions, and judgments. They're all outdated. Get to know the person that they currently are."*

—UNKNOWN

THE REINTRODUCTION PROCESS WAS A vital stage in my Delabeling Journey. From the time I made up in my mind that I could no longer, in a sense, be puppeteered and labeled by others, I knew it would be a time that I would become unrecognizable. People got used to the people-pleaser me, and the non-confrontational "if you like it I love it" girl. Most people were used to dealing with me on autopilot. The auto approach did not work for me anymore. I was vibrating higher from the place of the "yes" girl. I was doing the work to free myself from mental, spiritual, and emotional labels. I wanted more out of life. I started to walk in my own beliefs instead of ones that I followed blindly. I wanted to make my own family that accepted me for all of me instead of a family who tolerated me. My attitude and outlook were no longer the same. I wanted more. I needed more. I expected more. I also had to make these expectations known.

When I started breaking down what a reintroduction process would look like, one of my all-time favorite movies came to mind … *Antwone Fisher*. This touching movie depicted an emotional rollercoaster of events from a young sailor who experienced violent outbursts. He was sent to a naval psychiatrist for help but refused to comply initially. Eventually, the young man breaks down and reveals his horrific childhood traumas.

There are three central themes in this movie that were a huge inspiration in the way I approached the reintroduction process. In my discovery of effectively reintroducing myself, there were three important elements that stood out... Healthy Boundaries, Healthy Releasing, and Healthy Affirmations.

## Healthy Boundaries Part I – The Why?

After several sessions, Antwone Fisher's doctor encouraged him to confront his past by returning to the adopted family where he grew up. I could almost see as I watched the film, Antwone Fisher's Little Boy come to the forefront in fear as he refused to close the twenty-year gap to confront his past. This was the home where he was shamed, physically, and verbally abused by his adoptive mother, Mrs. Tate, and sexually assaulted and bullied by his adoptive cousin, Nadine. Despite his anxieties, he agreed that facing his past would be the first step in finding his birth mother.

In order to understand who he was, he needed to understand where he came from and possibly who he belonged to. He was ready and willing to take this step to heal the emotional infections that plagued him for far too long.

When Nadine opened the door, she recognized who Antwone was after a few seconds of passively greeting. She tried to embrace him with a welcoming hug because nothing had changed in her eyes, except for his age and height, but she was rejected. A few moments later, Mrs. Tate attempted the same type of embrace while simultaneously rebuking him for not visiting sooner and calling him the racial and demeaning slur they both used when Antwone was a child. After he rejected her greeting by pushing her arms back from trying to hug his neck, Antwone asserted, "This is my time! I remember everything, but I am still standing! I am strong and always will be!"

Now, that's setting boundaries! A boundary reminds me of a privacy fence that separates my physical space as well as my energy, feelings, and needs from others. In my quest to flourish in life, healthy boundaries were required to effectively communicate how I desired to be treated and what is and is not acceptable behavior and treatment in my presence. Antwone Fisher's story showed me the value of not allowing people in my space after they have become a repeat offender of abusive and neglectful behavior. Somewhere in my past, the adage "grin and bear it" stuck to me like gorilla glue. Accepting a difficult or unpleasant situation without complaining for the sake of people-pleasing and false peace was no longer an option for me.

My nickname, "the Peacemaker," was ripped off when I realized that this phrase was sending me down People Pleasing Lane. Boundaries are not about complying with someone else's needs. Setting healthy boundaries protected me from manipulation, verbal attacks, and emotional abuse.

When I confronted my verbal abuser, the first thing I made clear was, "I am not the same person I once was." I told her that there will be no manipulation by crying; there will be no raising of voices, or I will leave; and there will be no slandering, blaming, or shaming of myself and others. It was essential to state expectations upfront to protect my energy and space. In the same way, Antwone put an end to the perpetual abuse he endured until he was a teenager during one reintroduction of himself along with boundaries to ensure mental and emotional safety for himself.

**Hey, Little Girl:** Your name is no longer "Peace Maker."You now practice ensuring and securing your own peace.

**Hey, Dear Reader:** When you have encounters with your loved ones during the transformation process, they will look at you and see the same physical person, not recognizing the renovations that are going on within.

Just imagine a businesswoman working at a corporate office for ten plus years of her life. She knows what address to give the Uber driver and what the building will look like when she arrives. Every day she pauses to take in all of the building just before she enters. She knows to come through the revolving door and to proceed to the elevator, which is just past the elaborate floral centerpiece in the foyer. She knows to hit number sixteen because that's the floor her business is on. She knows to walk right when exiting the elevator to enter through the glass doors, greet the secretary that sits on the right, and proceed down to her office, which is positioned two doors down after the water cooler on the left. This businesswoman knows precisely what to do and what to expect when she comes to her place of business. She does all of this while checking her phone, sipping on her coffee, and without much thought.

Now, imagine that over the weekend, there was a last-minute renovation that she was not made privy to. Monday morning, the businesswoman hopped in the Uber and gave him the address. When she stepped out of the Uber, she looked at the building to take it all in as she usually would. Upon entering the building, she notices there is no revolving door, but an automatic double door instead. She steps back and looks at the address, which is the same and continues to look for the revolving door. She thinks the automatic door is an upgrade but insists on entering the building as she always did. She gets stuck yelling and complaining about her revolving door until the owner of the building explains that the changes for the glass automatic double door were a company decision to adhere to safety measures, for aesthetics, and for time efficiency.

Sometimes change confuses people. Some people in your life will acknowledge your change but still treat you the same. Do you presently get addressed by your nickname or experience others visiting your past more than you do? They don't realize that you not only do not live there anymore, but you also sold the whole building!

People will engage with you in the same manner as they always have if they do not discern your inner growth. As with the example above, there will be a time to have a conversation with those who expect the same thing out of you regardless of your Delabeling Journey. In many ways, people, especially family, feel like they have possession of you, which makes it hard to accept change even if they are directly faced with a new and improved version of you. You will know that the reintroduction process is necessary when (Check all that apply):

- You are the recipient of micro-aggression.

- People keep judging you and bringing up past situations that were forgiven or resolved from your past.

- When you have evolved from dependence to independence.

- When you have been released from a stronghold.

- When you are no longer a victim of your past.

- When you gave up the life of people pleasing.

- You are ready to implement boundaries or your current boundaries are not respected.

- When people still call you "Little Girl" but you are a whole-entire-grown woman.

Do any of these situations happen to you? If "yes," then it is time to instill some healthy boundaries. If "no" then make your own list of past labels you would like to dismantle for good. The key is to understand who you do not want to be addressed as and relay who you are today!

## Healthy Boundaries Part II–The What Ifs…

*"What if they do not like the new me?"* This question was a terrifying thought. This mindset kept me timid for a while when I started on my Delabeling Journey because, let's face it, people liked me for the labeled me. There was a possibility that people would not be open to getting to know someone new or be interested in the changes I have made in my life. Maybe my transformation is intimidating to them or serves as a mirror to the inner work they need to do but are not ready to do. My change may even trigger jealously and envy because the label did not do what it was supposed to do—like tear me down. But, then I have to remember that the work I have done and am still going to do is ALL about me. People will be receptive or not. People will be inspired or not.

*"What if my 'no' as a 'yes' girl is matched with a 'no' to continuing a relationship?"* I struggled with this question often. Losing friendships or having a fall out with a sibling was always traumatic for me. Enforcing the "no" boundary was a sure way to lose out on long-standing relationships. But that wasn't true for the significant relationships. I realized that my "no" to others was a "yes" to myself. Maya Angelou began to ring loud in my spirit: "You alone are enough. You have nothing to prove to anybody." The relationship I learned to nurture is the one with myself, first. Instead of thinking about "the what ifs," I shifted focus to just "if."

If I do not make myself a priority, I will fall back into making others a priority. Even if others do not like the new me, I like the evolved me. If my "no" is matched with others "no," then I just made room for someone with a "yes" to occupy that space. If I continued to worry around my potential losses, I would not have the energy to focus on my definite gains. I have gained freedom from boundaries. My boundaries saved my Little Girl from false impressions that have been placed on her to show up in the best way for my husband and children now and to position my future self for a bright, healthy, Delabeled future.

As the residue of the people-pleasing faded, and my concern for instilling healthy boundaries was in the forefront. I began to focus on those who applauded my bravery to up-level myself in my personal growth, instead of obsessing over the opinions of people who had self-fulfilling intentions. Like a metaphorical caterpillar processing into a butterfly, I was doing the work to unfold the best part of me. My biggest cheerleader and best friend, Maurice, who just so happens to be my amazing husband, sent me a text one day. It came at a time I least expected it, but at a time, I most needed to hear these words. (I got permission to share this text with you ladies.)

*You are strong and healthy. Your attitude often causes others around you to recognize their limitations, and they feel vulnerable. For a stronger/more secure person that is motivated to achieve self-actualization, the new you can be helpful to them. To an individual less secure, with low self-esteem, it causes them to bluster, leading them to retreat. This often presents in blaming, redirecting, and misplacing their anger on you. This is NOT your fault ... but only in the sense that you have made a significant change, and you as well as other people, need to recognize that you have entered a cocoon one way and exited another. No longer crawling slowly on the ground but proudly gliding confidently above your problems. While you can occasionally land at will, your mode of transportation has been upgraded to that of prestige. You're a 'Badass' chick. As long as you always remember that ... others will, too. I love you.*

**Hey, Little Girl:** First of all, Your. Husband. ROCKS! (And yes, I clapped between each word!). Second, you were too young to establish healthy boundaries, but now you are the Boundary Queen! You no longer have to concern yourself with predators. You are guarded by a supernatural fence that serves to protect your inner peace, joy, and worth. You have grabbed hold of that word "no" like it was the last chocolate chip cookie in the cookie jar. And you have embraced your "yes" because you desire to make your needs, your desires, and your dreams a priority.

**Hey, Dear Reader:** Teaching others how to respect your boundaries is essential and teaching yourself how to respect your boundaries is a game changer! Be uncompromising in protecting your boundaries and energy. The family who has known you all of your life or friends who have known you for many years are accustomed to who you always presented yourself as. Maybe you were always shy, your circle of friends know that you are not one to take chances or would never speak in public. Maybe you have been aggressive. Your family or friends are used to you saying what's on your mind and having a direct response. Perhaps you are a people pleaser, like me. Your friends or acquaintances may be used to you being a "yes" girl.

When you begin to speak up as the shy woman, become assertive as the aggressive woman, or have boundaries as the people pleaser, you become unrecognizable. But please remember: BOUNDARIES ARE A FORM OF SELF-LOVE. This is why the reintroduction process is so important. You are presenting your loved self to others, instead of your labeled person. Simply letting your close family and friends know about your evolution to becoming more of who you feel you desire to be, will help your loved ones get to know the new you. And the new you, with a hedge of beautiful floral adornments circling your energy's force, is one to be seen, respected, and appreciated by your Little Girl, your present self, and your elevated self!

## HEALTHY RELEASING

Antwone had another hard thing to do. When he found his father's side of the family, he was also made aware of his mother's whereabouts. Stepping into the very room where he longed to be since he could remember was bittersweet. He expressed how many times he longed for his mother to find him, take him for ice cream, and then take him home where he belonged. He expressed how he would imagine what she looked like, her scent, and the feel of her embrace. Yet, with everything that was said, this young man's mom was unresponsive. He poured out his heart to get silence in return.

People come into our lives to help us identify patterns, learn significant lessons, and evolve as humans. That being true, not all relationships are meant to last forever; some are only meant to last a season. When a relationship has consistent bad energy and becomes toxic, it is time to get out of harm's way. Releasing a relationship has its struggles, but I now listen to my trusted road dog—my gut, when it is time to let go. Some links are hard to break, like ones with family members or romantic relationships. But I do the incredibly hard work because NO ONE is worthy enough to strip us from our peace or steal our joy. Yet, as painful as the experience can be, there are healthy ways to release those relationships that are no longer serving you. Nevertheless, it is still challenging to detach from long-standing relationships.

Lisa Nicolas, aka Auntie Lisa, helped me emotionally settle the war in my spirit about ending and releasing people who were no longer for me. "Instead of thinking the relationship is over, think of the relationship as complete." The relationship has served its purpose, and while you will always have a degree of love for that complete relationship and even reminisce about what once was, it is ok to permit yourself to make room for a new and healthy relationship.

**Hey, Little Girl:** Many people could not love you the way you needed them to. We've talked about the reasons why. I want to assure you that now I always keep my invisible hands open. Open hands allow me to empathetically release those whose chapters are complete and receive those who are starting a new chapter with us. I am trusting the process, Little Girl, hard stuff, and all. I know that the people who care for us will manifest in ways that will continue to enlighten and help elevate us on our beautiful journey.

**Hey, Dear Reader:** It is okay if someone does not receive the new you. Other people have choices, too. Respect their decision and know their decision to move on from the relationship is no reflection on how dope you are becoming. Now, it may sting a bit, nope, it's going to sting a lot, but it is normal to feel sad about the loss. Mourn the loss of your loved one and allow them the grace to move forward. Maybe they do not have the capacity to get to know the new you. Or perhaps you are indirectly shaking something up in them that they are not ready to address. Don't judge them. Instead, remember that you once had a beginning point on your journey. So do they.

Healthy releasing is understanding that a relationship is not over—it is complete. Maybe you will reconnect with some, and perhaps you will not. The simple fact that your life's story involved them in some form or fashion means they impacted you in some way. Be emphatically appreciative of all they were and are to you and thank them for being honest, which is, in turn, the best thing for you. Never hold on to something that wants to be let go. Never try to stay where you are not welcomed anymore. It is okay.

Know that allowing someone to choose to leave a friend is allowing space for another divine connection for where you are now. Divine connections are to feed you now to help elevate you later. Remember, the people who are a part of your fleet will be there to push you into your divine destiny and encourage you to become more of your authentic self. Are you ready to release what is complete and receive what is to come? If you said, "Y.E.S.", let's pause right here and do a Delabeling exercise:

<table>
<tr><td align="center">Delabeling Exercise</td></tr>
<tr><td>

In an erected position, hold your hands up, palms facing one another, and make a Y with your arms as far as you can reach. Close your eyes and begin to think about all you want to release. Recite it for two minutes. Then, think about all you wish to receive to replace what you've just given. Recite it for two minutes. Then for thirty seconds, bask in the energy of what you just accepted, for the last thirty seconds, repeat, "I have received; I am expecting; I am grateful."

</td></tr>
</table>

## Healthy Labels/Affirmations – (Who I am now?)

Setting healthy boundaries and releasing labels and people is the work I did for my past and present self. Healthy labeling and affirmations were essential to vibrate my current self to a higher dimension. One of my favorite quotes that infiltrated my life was by my former online speaker's coach, Marshawn Evans-Daniels, "Every life shift begins with a mind shift." Read that again!

This one thought inspired a brand new belief system in me. "I can think myself happy … think myself worthy … think myself successful." Of course, it is more than just a thought, there is implementation, but all things begin with an idea! Just think about the technology devices you use daily. That cell phone, that laptop, those wireless earbuds were just a thought. So, if a dream of a communication device can turn into a worldwide phenomenon, then my inner thoughts and labels can become a manifestation of a Super Elevated Me!

There are so many mind moving benefits of healthy labels and affirmations. During this process, I realized that…

- Healthy labels and affirmations motivated me to act.

- Healthy labels and affirmations helped me to concentrate on my goals.

- Healthy labels and affirmations changed my negative thought patterns into positive ones.

- Healthy labels and affirmations influenced my subconscious mind to access new beliefs.

- Healthy labels and affirmations helped me to feel positive about myself and boost my self-confidence.

- Healthy labels and affirmations were great practices to make positive labels permanent!

**Hey, Little Girl:** I affirm that you are loved, you are seen, you are heard, you are worthy, you are mentally and emotionally well, you are wanted, you are worthy, you are creative, you are intelligent, you are ENOUGH and you always have been!

**Hey, Dear Reader:** In Chapter 3, you unveiled the lies and embraced the truth of who you really are. Now, it is time for you to do the same with healthy affirmations. It is so important to start your day in a positive mind space! Positive thoughts create positive energy. Positive energy creates positive experiences. Positive experiences generate a positive lifestyle.

It may feel weird at first but talk to yourself while feeling weird. Also, embody your words with incantations because affirmations are psychological as well as physical. Singing, dancing, posture, smiling, voice volume, hand gestures and standing tall when affirming yourself help produce a heightened level of confidence and believability. It is okay if you look silly. Silly is fun and the Little Girl in you will love it!

Remember that practice doesn't make perfect, practice makes permanent! I can't even tell you when my mind-shift happened. One day, I was thinking differently, responding differently, seeing myself and others through new lenses of love. But it started with affirming myself in love, grace, and patience first. You have a voice, Dear Reader, speak life into yourself now!

One of the exercises that was helpful, and fun was the Instagram Labeling Challenge I saw on my cousin's page. An example of my image is on the following page. Now it's your turn!

## Delabeling Exercise

For this exercise we are going to switch it up with some labeling ... positive labeling of course!

Do this five-minute exercise and have fun with it. List ten "I am" statements about yourself in the boxes that surrounds the outlined woman on the following page. You can cut and paste a picture of yourself on the outlined woman or make as many copies as you would like to repeat the activity. As you revisit this exercise, some of the labels will change because you will continue to evolve. The objective is not to let a specific label define you, but to allow affirmations to remind you of who you are becoming every day!

Note: If you need help with thinking of some powerful affirmation statements, there is a list of "I am" statements in the back of this book.

# I affirm that...

My life is full of prosperity and blessings.

My words heal, inspire, and transform!

I am treasured for who I really am.

I radiate confidence!

I AM ENOUGH!

I give and receive love equally…

I am surrounded by love!

I am overflowing with happiness, joy, and satisfaction.

Peace is my birthright!

I am healthy, energetic, and optimistic.

I am teachable and a life learner.

# I affirm that...

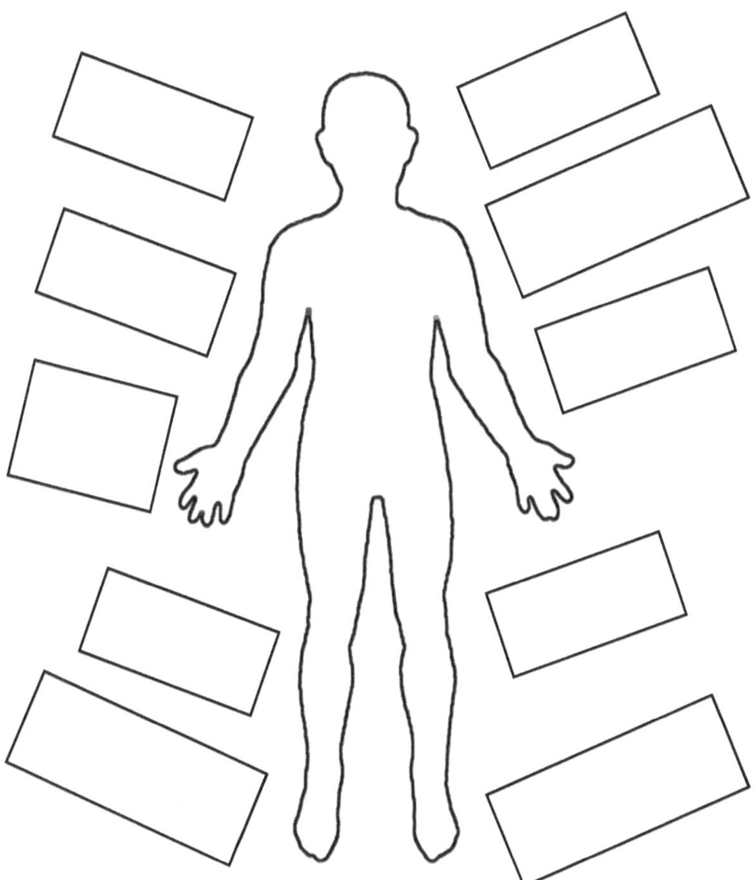

# CHAPTER 10: RELAPSE VS. RESET

**(Step Nine in the Delabeling Process)**

*"Hit the reset button 1000 times, and then hit it again!"*
– Lisa Nicholas

I WAS LOYAL TO A fault. I was so desperate to have and keep friends and to find my place in life that I would ignore the signs that nudged me to run away from toxic relationships. Even when I would adhere to the warning signs, I would second guess myself or judge myself, thinking I was being unreasonable. Before I started my Delabeling Process, I began to see patterns of abuse in relationships albeit verbally or emotionally. I didn't fully understand narcissism at that time so, as an empath, people with narcissistic traits had me for breakfast, lunch, dinner, and a snack.

I remember crying to my husband one day, asking what am I doing so wrong? "I forgive and forget. I try to be a good friend. I…" That would go on for hours. I was desperate to understand how to have a thriving relationship while not compromising my beliefs and way of being. And I have to note that because of labels, I am sure I sabotaged some relationships because of my low self-worth. I now know that it is impossible to love others if I don't love myself first.

The heartache of being reinjured, oftentimes by the same individual, was because I would have the mindset that everyone should get the benefit of the doubt. I still believe that people are human and will make human mistakes, including myself. But I took "benefit of the doubt" to mean swallowing my feelings and dealing with other people's invalidating disposition. I would go back to a relationship with open emotional wounds to only get infected by rumination and anxiety. I began to realize that I was addicted to acceptance and belonging. So, what would really happen when I go back to an unhealthy relationship is a relapse.

When someone relapses, the first thought that comes to mind is a worsening medical condition or restarting an addictive behavior. Similarly, as an intransitive verb, Webster's dictionary definition of relapse is to slip or fall back into a former worse state or practice. When it comes to labeling, *relapse* is defined as continuously getting stuck in an emotionally unhealthy space due to having a false sense of identity, worth and appreciation for one-self.

I would always be in danger of relapsing if I continued to put time and attention into others, instead of focusing on myself. If I did not come to grips with the fact that I do not need others to validate my being, I would be in trouble for an emotional and mental pitfall. This is a sure way to fall into depression. This is a guaranteed way to kill any chance of rediscovering myself outside of the labels I have lived with for so long. I needed to do something different. I needed to dig deep and figure out what I needed to be happy. I needed to let go. I needed to **RESET!**

**Hey, Little Girl:** The life choices I made and the treatment I allowed from others had to be scary to you. Your seated position on the ground was an illustration of the times I dismissed my feelings and needs. You were showing me what it meant to be energetically stuck in time. Time kept going, but along the way there was a trail of myself at different ages mired in much mental suffering and sadness. You reappearing was a way to bring negative behavioral patterns to my attention. Once I stopped projecting my frustrations out on the vision of you and was brave enough to love on you, you did something miraculous. You got up!

Standing up during that therapy session symbolized a resetting. All you needed was validation from me that you were always enough. Well you are, Little Girl! Through your repositioning, I, too, have repositioned. I do not wait for validation from others, I validate myself … I am patient with myself … I forgive myself … I love myself! Most of all, I am cultivating emotional intelligence. I am putting my feelings in its rightful place and using life and a lesson. I am allowing myself to be happy. I am making you my dance partner, Little Girl, as I reset from tracing others' footsteps into two-stepping to the beautiful sound of our future.

**Hey, Dear Reader:** There is value in honoring your feelings and then hitting the R.E.S.E.T (Re-Examine Sinister Elephant Troubles) button at all times. Elephants can seem intimidating because of their stature, but in essence elephants are mostly altruistic and harmless. We have to ask ourselves … when "elephant troubles" stomp us down, do they come to crush us, or can you find ways to learn from the situation and aid your elevated self?

Of course we have real significant troubles that arise in life. Some things are simply out of our control. But then we have some things that are in our control. Situations that arise may not be as big and scary as they seem. In many cases, when we re-examine problematic situations, we are able to learn important lessons, which makes the situation less threatening. It is good to have this type of re-evaluating after having a bad day or week. The ability to reset is the safest road to travel on your Delabeling Journey. But, like any smart traveler, we need to map out our understanding of the road ahead, so let us briefly examine the avenues of what resetting is and what resetting is not.

**RESETTING IS** about feeling your feelings and letting go of the notion that you are weak if you respect and accept your emotions. Resetting is what the late musical artist, Aaliyah, sang about, *"At first you don't succeed, dust yourself off and try again."* Resetting is letting go of old habits and former thought processes and grabbing hold of new ideas that elevate you.

**RESETTING IS NOT** starting over in unhealthy or abusive relationships. Resetting is not adjusting to someone else's ideas of you or their will for your life. Resetting is not dimming your light so others will not be intimidated by the fire you possess inside.

Knowing the difference between relapsing and resetting is important. It is easy to get confused with what's going on with you emotionally if you don't realize having a bad day is normal. If you do not appropriate your feelings, you will relapse out of frustration, intimidation, and even stress.

## WHY DO WE RELAPSE?

### *Trauma Bonds*

Sherry Gaba, LCSW, a licensed psychotherapist and life

coach, explains how trauma bonds can lead to relapse:

*Within a trauma bond, the narcissist's partner—who often has codependency issues—first feels loved and cared for. However, this begins to erode over time, and the emotional, mental, and sometimes physical abuse takes over the relationship.*

*The codependent understands the change, but not why it is occurring. They believe they just need to understand what they are doing wrong in order to bring back the loving part of the relationship.*

*If they do manage to break free, all the narcissist has to do is go back to that courtship phase to win them back. The more the codependent reaches out to the narcissist for love, recognition, and approval, the more the trauma bond is strengthened. This also means the codependent will stay in the relationship when the abuse escalates, creating a destructive cycle.*

Gaba breaks down how codependency has the ability to spiral out of control if we do not hit the R.E.S.E.T button. Having unhealthy emotional ties only pulls us down. This is why ridding our past labels are so vital to our survival. Do not allow anyone … I mean ANYONE to hold you back from reaching your truest identity. Seeking a professional therapist or life coach will help you with separating from the toxic relationship, acknowledge and accept the part you play in relationships as well as affirm making better choices, and developing a network of supporters (your Fleet of S.H.I.Ps) as you journey forward.

## Imposter Syndrome

According to research, "Imposter Syndrome is a psychological pattern in which an individual doubts their skills, talents or accomplishments and has a persistent internalized fear of being exposed as a 'fraud.'"

People with imposter syndrome do not think they are worthy of their marriage, career, or any success, thus the reason they self-sabotage and fall back into unhealthy habits or relationships. All of us who are high achievers experience imposter syndrome on some level. There may be a feeling of not belonging in a certain social space or job, for example, for fear of failing and being found out as unqualified. I certainly dealt with a form of imposter syndrome during this writing process. *"Who am I to try to help women become Delabeled when there are so many books on the same subject or more successful people out there talking about the importance of finding your identity?"* That was one of many thoughts. But then I had to ask another question: *"Who am I not to share my story to help other women who are sick of being haunted by their past? I am more than qualified to be in this space… It's my story!"*

You see, we can easily gravitate to feeling like an impostor when we are not focused on the seemingly big deals of life. The real deal is that a R.E.S.E.T mindset will keep you in truth about you. It will keep you from back tracking into former thoughts of who you once were. Pressing that mental R.E.S.E.T button helps keep you from accepting judgement from others and judging yourself. You belong in your space without permission. If there is a persistent feeling of imposter syndrome, again, seek professional assistance to help you better cope with your feelings. If I did not say this before, I will say it now, seeking help is a form of self-care. So, take care of you!

## Upper Limits

Learning about "upper limits" gives a great understanding of why we relapse. Gay Hendricks, author of *The Big Leap*, illustrates that:

> *'The Upper Limit Problem' is a negative emotional reaction that occurs when anything positive enters our lives. 'The Upper Limit Problem' not only prevents happiness, but it actually stops us from achieving our goals. It is the ultimate life roadblock.*

What would you do if you ran into a roadblock on your way to something important? Probably turn around and travel the road you just came from looking for a detour, right? Similar to this instance, when we run into a big problem or "elephant troubles" we are likely to relapse into the same situation we were previously in. But most of the time we are not capable of detouring out of that situation if we do not feel we desire happiness or are worthy of achieving goals. Hendricks goes on to illustrate that:

> *Each of us has an inner thermostat setting that determines how much love, success, and creativity we allow ourselves to enjoy. When we exceed our inner thermostat setting, we will often do something to sabotage ourselves, causing us to drop back into the old, familiar zone where we feel secure. Unfortunately…*

This is a very real description of why we get comfortable existing. But when you hit the R.E.S.E.T button, you are saying that I will no longer just exist in the temperature that someone set for me, I will adjust my own temperature to the highest setting until I break free and the degree of my temperature reads **"LIMITLESS!"**

## DOS AND DON'TS

To avoid relapsing it is helpful to understand what old habits do not elevate you forward. We experience many situations where we will have to make decisions based on our new outlook on life. With your new outlook, comes new behavior. But remember, practice makes permanent! The chart below shows a few examples of how to recover when you relapse. After reading the examples, write down some of your own ways to navigate relapsing and resetting.

| Examples | **Relapse:** What Not to Do… | **Reset:** What to Do… |
| --- | --- | --- |
| Business idea failed… | • Give Up<br>• Beat yourself up | • Try another innovative idea<br>• Seek wise counsel from peers or professionals in the same industry |
| Some impose their unsolicited opinion… | • Respond with aggression<br>• Ignore them | • Reply with assertiveness<br>• Know what others think of you is none of your business |
| Physically and mentally exhausted with everyday life… | • Run on fumes<br>• Push through the warning signs to rest | • Recharge with meditation<br>• Recharge with a self-care day |
| Conflict in a relationship… | • Use language that you will regret later<br>• Blame, shame, or assign guilt | • Talk to your Coach or Therapist to gather tools that will assist with healthy communication<br>• Apologize if necessary |
| Mess up on a work or personal project… | • Negative self-talk<br>• Ruminate | • Exercise self-compassion, love, and forgiveness<br>• Learn from the mistake and start again with grace |

## THE POWER OF RESETTING

The power of resetting is that you start to take your marching orders from your future self, instead of being dictated by your past. Those "elephant troubles" we talked about can reoccur so much that we get used to being stomped on and crushed under so much weight. But being crushed, in a figurative sense, is not so bad with the right perception and discernment (I will touch more on this in the next chapter). For now, know that hitting that R.E.S.E.T button doesn't just start you over, it starts you anew. Restarting is doing something again the same way, but resetting is showing up differently in a more positive way.

If you are not resetting, you are relapsing. And in the voice of Ms. Sweet Brown, "Ain't nobody got time for that!" The only option has to be forwardness. There is no getting ready for all the promises our future holds if we don't bounce back when we fall. And let's just say, we will fall, but that doesn't mean we will stay down. With every R.E.S.E.T, there is a new confidence, a new boldness, and a new readiness to use that hard surface as a bouncing board. We will learn from those "elephant troubles," and put that threat of fear in its place. There is no room for us on the ground. It's time for us to start anew and push forward to advance to our rightful place.

Our rightful place is the destination of knowing who

you are and living in the enchantment of your true identity. Our rightful place lives in our Y.E.S.!

<table>
<tr><td align="center">Delabeling Exercise</td></tr>
</table>

As we get our hands ready to slam down on that R.E.S.E.T button, think about this:

1. What are some things that are causing you to relapse?

2. What do I want to R.E.S.E.T to? (a new career, new relationship, home, etc.) Keep a journal of where you are resetting to and add details of how to sustain that R.E.S.E.T. When it comes down to it, follow Lisa Nicholas' advice and hit that R.E.S.E.T button 1000 times if you need to … and then hit it again!

# CHAPTER 11: SAY "Y.E.S."!

## (Step ten of the Delabeling Process)

*"Once you SAY YES, all things will work together for your good and for your goals."*

-STACIA PIERCE

MY SISTER-IN-LAW AND I HAD our first vision board party in January 2020 called "Dream It, Work It, Live It." Like-minded women came together to dream big again. It is easy for life to get in the way, but in that moment we made a pact with one another to say "YES" to working smarter not harder to bring our dreams to fruition. That evening we shared, we cried, we laughed, we planned, and we created vision boards that represented what the year 2020 would look like for us. Everyone left refreshed and ready to execute the plans they set before them.

The vision board party was so powerful that my sister-in-law and I thought it would be great to stay connected. So a Facebook Group was created called "Say **Y.E.S.**" (**Y**our **E**levated **S**elf) with the objective of encouraging one another and celebrating milestones together.

Little did we know our "Y.E.S." year seemed to be bulldozed over by a big fat "NO" when a global pandemic hit. For the first few months, I can only imagine that everyone's hopes and dreams were turned upside down. This pandemic was nothing anyone could see coming, but everyone was simultaneously affected by. From April to June, my inner will to dream anything started to flee. The realization of what was really going on started to take a toll on my mental health. I would look at my vision board wondering how my dreams would manifest and more importantly would I be alive to fulfill them.

When July came around, I suddenly felt the determination to recommit to my "Y.E.S." It was my birthday month, and it was also time to focus. My new chapter in life meant new beginnings. Even in the midst of a pandemic, turmoil, or hardship, I said "Y.E.S." to a new perspective. Before the pandemic, I was always super busy. Once I allowed myself to view this pandemic as a new opportunity, I remembered that my "Y.E.S." was an agreement with your future self to keep going in spite of it! So, in July I decided to start fulfilling one of my dreams and that was to become an author. I believe everyone has a story in them that can uplift and inspire someone. So, I decided to look at July as the start of an incubation period instead of a lockdown period.

Incubation is scary from the outside looking in, but it is also a necessary developmental time to grow and mature. It was also a time to gain spiritual nutrition through meditation, prayer, and reading. While being alone, in a sense, used to be a fear, I started to appreciate the time to recharge and reframe my "Y.E.S." The work of becoming elevated in all manners was no longer romanticized. To say "Y.E.S." took examination, dedication, and a commitment to my highest levels of my being.

The saying: "What you do today, reflects who you will be tomorrow" was like refueling an empty gas tank. I put it on a Post-it and stuck it on my desk along with my other collage of sayings. Even though the walls on the outside still felt like they were closing in with everything that was going on with the world today, I had hope that there would be a brighter tomorrow. I believed that after the storm, the sun would shine, and I wanted to be ready to go out and seize any opportunity to help women remove the labels that duct taped them for far too long so they, too, can say "Y.E.S."

**Hey, Little Girl:** Do you remember your reaction when you received that grey stuffed animal for Christmas when you were eight years old? You fell in love with that mouse/bear looking thing. You slept with it, you played with it, and you even named it Sean. Thirty-three years later, we still have that same stuffed animal with one less eye. I gifted it to my son, whose name is … Sean! You see, some gifts are to be treasured and passed on because they are so special. The gift of life is extremely special and one I have learned to treasure each day.

My "Y.E.S." is to show gratitude to God because life is not owed to us, it is given to us as a gift. My "Y.E.S." is also making a pact with myself to reach all of the silly and big dreams in my future. You are now living your dream of becoming a dancer and together we will offer the gift of our story to other women so their Little Girl will be free to dance, too.

**Hey, Dear Reader:** If there is one thing we all can agree on, it is the fact that life will happen. That means there will be hiccups, and pitfalls, and holdups, and devastating times that have the ability to crush us on every side. But the crushing does not have to destroy you. The pressure can make you stronger. In T.D. Jakes' book *Crushing: God Turns Pressure into Power*, he asked, "We may not like to admit it, but what if our crushing is necessary in order for our potential to be fulfilled?" When I thought about the answer, I began to think about how wine is made.

The crushing process is the most important part of making wine. With every step it flattens the grape more and more, squeezing everything valuable out to make fine wine. It is a messy process, but the time and energy put in to crush all of the juice out of each grape is needed to prepare it for fermentation.

Just like the making of wine, we have felt crushed on all sides especially in the year 2020. With the effects of the Covid-19 pandemic on many lives … increased violence, high unemployment rates, fighting for equality among races, the loss of influential giants, and an unimaginable presidential election … 2020 has been relentless! We have been tried and uprooted from what was "normal" into what seems like chaos. But what we also got from 2020 is a new level of creativity and resilience!

The tighter the squeeze, the more innovative we became. Every execution was not perfect or easy, somehow with every "stomp" we were able to produce more valuable ways to work together and survive. School staff learned how to work closely with parents to start virtual learning, companies resorted to zoom meetings to keep businesses afloat, and citizens donated to food pantries to ensure no child goes hungry during an unprecedented time.

The idea of being flattened, stomped, or squeezed is not appealing, but we can now see how the crushing process is what you make it. In the toughest times in history, many of us are coming out of our incubation period stronger and more buoyant than ever. The fermentation process can last three days or three months, and the wine can then mature for a couple of weeks or a couple of years or anything in between. No matter how long it takes, you have the power to get clear on what your life will look like in spite of what's going on around you. It is easier to notice a crushing "no." But, it is life changing to focus your EYES … so you will always see your "Y.E.S!"

## WHAT ARE YOU SAYING "Y.E.S." TO?

> *"When the Master gives us the vision of what*
> *he's going to do in our lives, He shows us the*
> *mountain peaks while He hides the valleys.*
> *If you saw the climb you would have to*
> *endure to get to the mountaintop,*
> *you would abandon the entire trip."*
>
> -T.D. JAKES

Saying "Y.E.S." is like a rollercoaster ride. You are anxious as you stand in line to wait your turn on a new ride. You are nervous as you are strapped in. You have great anticipation to reach the top, clenching to the safety bars, convincing yourself that this was a great decision. As you reach the top of the hill, you say a prayer, but before you say "amen" your cart drops 100 miles per hour on this narrow track jerking your body all over the place with every turn.

Yes, a roller coaster ride is thrilling but can also feel like you dislocated parts of your limbs after the ride.

Life's journey can be unpredictable and there are times when you will want to ask to get off the ride. This is when you need to let go of your need to know what's going to happen next and trust the process.

Your "Y.E.S." means:

1.  You agree to the thrill of the venture and will find ways to endure when it gets scary
2.  You will value your uniqueness and make room for all of your creativity to unfold the best parts of you.
3.  You will always Dream It, Work It, and Live It to the best of your ability and realm of   expertise.
4.  You will glean from your Fleet of S.H.I.Ps    to run from a full vessel instead of teaching from an empty vessel.
5.  You will cultivate a legacy of "Y.E.S."ers through your children and every woman and Little Girl that seeks to soar to endless bounds.

## WHEN YOU SAY "Y.E.S."

The next time you see a bird fly away, follow it to see how far it will ascend. Then think of that bird as yourself and allow your imagination to wonder what altitude you are able to reach when you keep saying "Y.E.S." When you say "Y.E.S."

you can go as far as you want to grab hold of the possibilities of a promising future.

SAY "Y.E.S." to being free as a bird. When a caged bird sees an open door, it does not hesitate to fly free. I do not care how long that bird has been captured. Its innate knowledge of what it is automatically seeks an opening to escape a caged life. Birds were created to spread their wings and fly. So were you, Dear Reader, so fly, Birdie, fly!

## <u>"Y.E.S." UNIVERSITY ALUMNI</u>

"Because of me continuing to say YESSS … Shoes for Your Soul Nonprofit Children Shoe Organization is blessing many children with new and gently used shoes along with new socks in Camden County, Dominican Republic and Ghana!!! Just say YESSS … to God's will!"

– Dawn Lewis, shoesforyoursoul.org

"2020 has been a crazy year! Covid-19 halted a business idea that my husband and I were pursuing to manifest this past summer. However, that did not stop me. My 'Y.E.S.' catapulted me to resume my writing and now I am an author! I am grateful and excited knowing that my book will restore HOPE to many." -Tanya Taylor

"I said 'Y.E.S.' to expanding my brand for my former business, Syreetacreeations, and am saying 'Y.E.S.' again to starting a new business venture that I am truly excited to begin and see it prosper!" – Syreeta Swain

IG: @syreetascreeations AND

@sjsvendingenterprisellc

"I said, 'Y.E.S.' to committing myself to being closer to Jesus like never before. It impacted me because I learned how Jesus sees me, the REAL ME! I'm able to be my true authentic self and I have peace that surpasses all understanding!" – Myking Johnson

"With my 'Y.E.S,' I created a new inspirational merchandise line that inspires people to live their best life. JGJI Inspo Merch wardrobe will remind people to trust the process, evolve, grow and vibrate higher!"
– Jennifer Gregg, IG: @jgji_inspo

"I was frustrated and disappointed in life, but my 'Y.E.S.' helped me focus on up leveling my spiritual life through prayer, meditation, and reading more. I am now intentionally living a spiritual life that will glorify God and my elevated self!" – Alexis Mitchell

# CHAPTER 12: STAYING DELABELED

## (The Everyday Journey)

*"Use your power of your word in the direction of truth and love."*

—Don Miguel Ruiz

I READ *THE FOUR AGREEMENTS* by Don Miguel Ruiz during a time when I was feeling label-free bliss after doing the hard work of shedding my labels. I felt like a whole new person after walking those ten steps and I felt accomplished and ready to live in my true identity. After reading *The Four Agreements,* I realized that the journey of being Delabeled never ends. The everyday steps as a person free of labels takes on a new role with new endeavors and that is, agreeing to be impeccable with my words, don't take anything seriously, don't make assumptions, and always do my best. After reading this book a couple times, I realized that as a Delabeled woman, I had the responsibility to not only make an agreement with myself, but an agreement with all of the Little Girls that I saw in my Little Girl's face that day during the Empty Chair Exercise.

I was not sure what I was seeing then, but what my Little Girl was showing me was that we are similar in so many ways as women. We may all have a different story, but we all have been energetically stuck in various places at various ages throughout life. My Little Girl was showing me that what we have in common is the desire to be seen, healed, and free. Seen, Healed, Free … WOW! As I am typing right now, I realize that this was what the three phases really represented.

- Being seen caused my Little Girl to look up.

- Accepting love in that place of hurt healed my Little Girl.

- Feeling free led to a freedom dance!

That is what all women aspire to: being seen, being healed, and being free! With years of dealing with sexism and discrimination as a woman, I would be more intentional not to add to another woman's trauma again. This does not mean I will not get it wrong sometimes, this only means that I will do what is within my control to "use my power of my words in the direction of truth and love" in hopes to free other Little Girls within.

**Hey, Little Girl:** Just when I thought I was done, I realized I have only just begun. I literally had a "aha" moment as I was sharing our story. I thought I had it before, but I got it now. Your phases of being represented three specific elements that I desired all of my life … Being Seen, Being Healed, and Being Free! The bonus in all of this is knowing that you are free and that has given me the fire I needed to not only write this book but continue the work of Delabeling one inner Little Girl at a time. If our story causes even one other woman's Little Girl who is energetically stuck to LOOK UP, TAKE A STAND, and DANCE FREE, it would be worth all that we have been through.

I appreciate your strength and tenacity, Little Girl, because it got us to accept our true identity, and it will keep us moving into our "Y.E.S."! I love you, Little Girl… Thank you!

**Hey, Dear Reader:** Don Miguel Ruiz teaches us that **our words matter**. And not only our words, but our behaviors and our thoughts matter. Our thoughts are oftentimes manifested in our words and behaviors. This is why those affirmations are so important. Remember, affirmations are more than words; it is psychological and it is physical. If positivity in word and deed become integrated into our vernacular, we will do our best to avoid labeling ourselves again, and labeling others. When you are labeled, that negativity shines light on imperfections causing insecurities in our lives. Although we all have imperfections, breaking the cycle of labeling ourselves and others is crucial to staying Delabeled. When you realize that you are gossiping, thinking negative thoughts about yourself or others, or have lost your cool, just hit the R.E.S.E.T button.

Staying Delabeled is remembering that you are human and will do human things—like mess up. Staying Delabeled is not being perfect, it is being aware and intentional. Practice does not make perfect, practice makes permanent! So, acknowledge the times you do label someone, apologize, forgive yourself, and give it another shot.

It takes a lifetime to stay Delabeled … that's a great thing, by the way. You never want to see yourself as "arrived." Always see yourself as "arriving" to keep you excited about the journey. There are many new and thrilling destinations ahead of you. So keep going!

In this bonus chapter, I want to share three last nuggets to help you stay Delabeled:

1. DON'T LABEL YOURSELF, and if you accidently do, snatch that label off like a bandage. That sting will teach you when you think about doing it the next time.

• Resist negative talk. Your brain will receive and

believe what you say about yourself more so than anyone else.

- Resist drawing conclusions about yourself.

*Client: "I am impulsive because I usually leave people who hurt me this bad."*

*Me: "Impulsive means acting emotionally or without forethought. Self-worth means knowing one's own value. Do you leave because you are emotionally charged, or do you leave because you know you deserve better?"*

The latter explanation was her truth. If she would have continued to draw inappropriate conclusions about herself, she would have never been freed from the burden of impulsivity.

2. DON'T LET OTHER PEOPLE'S LABELS STICK. The reality is, we do not have control over what others do. There are so many quotes in social media that confirm this point like… *"What others think or say about you is none of your business."* But even Miguel doubled downed on this notion with his brilliant advice: *"Whatever happens around you, don't take it personally… Nothing other people do is because of you. It is because of themselves."*

The point is, do not allow what others say to penetrate because, more than likely, it's not about you. Act as if you still use baby oil to moisturize your body and let that label slide right off. (If you still use baby oil to moisturize, do you, no judgement here!) Now, it is ok to quickly examine if what is said has any validity. If so, own your part, get it right with the other party and yourself, and keep it moving. If not, hit the reject button and eject any labels out of your space of peace. No matter what, NO LIMITING LABELS ALLOWED. Remember this, *"When you finally learn that a person's behavior has more to do with their own internal struggle than it ever did with you … you learn grace."*

3. DON'T LABEL OTHERS – *"Sticks and stones may break my bones, but words will never hurt me."* Do you remember that childhood chant? Well, somebody lied to us! Words do hurt and it is a powerful tool that can keep us energetically stuck. And like I said early, our words matter.

That's why I love the agreement to be impeccable with your word. Try to talk slower and think faster before saying anything, especially in a confrontation. Adults have to be impeccable with their words toward our youth. Children have to be taught and reminded to be impeccable with their words toward siblings, peers, and adults. This goes for the Boss Woman/Man … Employees … Government Leaders … Citizens … you get the point!

We all have to exercise more restraint with labeling others if we will to live free of labels. This may seem like a huge feat, but it only takes one person at a time. As they say, Rome was not built in one day. Together we can build each other up.

## IT'S NOT GOODBYE, IT'S WELCOME TO THE DELABELED LIFE!

I hope by now you realize that this is not a "get over it" process. This is not a "just suck it up" book. No, we have heard both demands time and time again for far too long. This is a book that helps women get their Little Girls unstuck and free from past lies and labels. This is a book to help you choose a new guide instead of being led by a compass of hurts that were in the driver seat of past behaviors and thought patterns. Recognizing our past labels is the reason we can now understand who we do not want to be and who we are destined to be.

Reading this book does not mean you have been dislodged from every stuck place. It does mean you agree to keep journeying forward to "Y.E.S." It means you are cultivating the life you want for yourself. It means you are constructing a new palace to live in as you take residence in the Delabeled Life!

In this life, you're going to have some days where you want to take refuge from the hustle. But, once you get a taste of what's possible, there is no going back. In this life, choose to show up for yourself consistently and consciously every day. Equally important, teach others what is possible in this Delabeled Life.

In this life, we do not subscribe to anything that is not uplifting, lovely, peaceful, or transformative. In this life, we understand that self-awareness is key to unlocking the door to someone's past labels. An apology goes a long way to helping someone realize that you were wrong and are working on getting better. We accept the challenge of monitoring our own insecurities and projections with the ability to call our own selves out with grace and compassion. This new living space is made up of mirrored walls as a reminder that what we say and do to others is a reflection of who we are. Our lives have been upgraded, we are living the Delabeled Life!

## A Delabeled Life Poem

You have **Identified the Labels** that you have lived with so long.

Now, you **Embrace the Truth** and know that those **Unveiled Lies** were wrong.

The process of **Forgiveness** is for all parties to be released and un-cuffed.

But do not be tempted to journey on with **The Mask** because the beauty of who you are is enough!

Commit to **Just B.E,** which is becoming and evolving into the best version of you.

It's ok to **Focus on Yourself!** How do you do that? I'll give you a clue.

Cultivate love from within until you see the Warrior Woman you are.

Your **Fleet of S.H.I.Ps** will fight off any adverse past labels and help you say, "au revoir."

A **Reintroduction Process** may be in favor, but you will know if that's required.

Some will resist and some will hate, but most will be inspired.

This journey can be weary, so you have a choice to **Relapse or R.E.S.E.T.**

You will always bounce back, Dear Reader, and exuberantly **Say, "Y.E.S."**!

## Dear Brother

This book has been an emotional rollercoaster to say the least. On one hand, I was excited and overcome with joy to have the opportunity to help other women who are haunted by the labels of their past. The freedom to live in my true identity is one I wanted every woman on this earth to know. On the other hand, grief hovered and weighed on my chest making it hard to catch my breath and think clearly. It saddens me that you never had a chance to fully heal from your past traumas. You didn't have your chance to truly be free. I wish I had just a few more moments to share some meaningful and memorable stories that happened throughout this healing journey, but I don't. The thing is, I had a chance to journey through a Delabeling Process that yielded so many great benefits that I wish you were able to experience so you, too, could have been whole.

As I talked to my Little Girl and the Little Girls of many other women throughout this book, I realized that you never had an opportunity to address your Little Boy. I wish there was a healing process that you could have gone through to experience your own liberation. That is what makes it so hard to truly embrace this accomplishment. It is a bitter-sweet experience because I couldn't call you and I couldn't write to you ... you are no longer here.

Here is what I wanted to tell you, and this is what I did...

I made an appointment with Dr. Sharon, a week after submitting my manuscript to the editor. This appointment was much different because it was virtual due to the pandemic … yes, you heard me right … we are in the midst of a global pandemic as I write! During our talk, I expressed a sense of guilt and unresolvedness in my spirit. I explained that though you apologized, and I accepted, I resisted sharing the pain of my childhood in fear of upsetting you or messing up our bonding moment. Without voicing the debt of grief, the reconciliation was not fully complete, leaving a void and unfinished business in me.

As Dr. Sharon shared her insight, she asked, "If your brother were here today, would you share your heart with him?"

I answered, "Yes," and immediately felt my head slowly falling to my chest as a cloud of sadness filled the room like a thick fog. The realization of you not being here hit me hard.

To tell you the truth, I do not think I grieved your death properly in an attempt to be strong for the family. Suddenly, my chest got heavy and a rush of warmth filled my face. As I was focused on fighting back the tears, the room fell quiet, because the Dr. paused mid-sentence and asked, *"Do you want to do it again?"*

I looked up at the screen and asked, *"Do what again?"*

She replied, *"The Empty Chair Exercise."*

My mouth immediately dried up like a desert and I could suddenly hear my heart beat as loud as a drum. I stumbled over every word that was trying to escape my mouth. *"Ummm, I mean … do I … so do it again … I was just calling to … I don't know…"* I took a deep breath and replied, *"Maybe I should."*

Silence took over the room as Dr. Sharon covered her screen so it would be just you and me. I sunk back into the pillows on my bed and pulled the blanket close as a source of safety. My eyes swelled up immediately as I closed them … tears flowed like a quiet stream. I honestly did not know where or how to start so I waited to possibly feel your presence, but there was nothing. So, I took a deep breath in and breathed out slowly.

*"Hey, Big Brother. First, I want to say I love you very much. I am so sorry that you are gone. I wish I could turn back the hands of time, but I can't. I wish we had more time, but we don't. I need a moment to connect with you because I am finally ready to remove this last label that I did not realize was still stuck on me. The label that read 'fear of you.'*

*"I want to let you know that I walked away from our conversation when you apologized long ago with forgiveness in one hand and fear in the other. Right now I am letting all fear go. I am sorry that your Little Boy never got all that he needed to feel truly safe and loved. I wish you had a chance to go back to talk to your Little Boy and free yourself. I wish you had more opportunities*

*to become the man I know you could have been with all of your innate gifts and talents.*

*"I understand why things happened, not excusing your behavior because you had a choice to make as well. I just want you to know that I truly understand. I hope you understand me as well. I am grateful that all the past pain experienced has turned into a process of healing. Not only healing but change in our family.*

*"To be transparent, I almost did not write this book because I do not want anyone viewing you in a negative light. I also was afraid that I would be viewed adversely for sharing my story that included my dead brother. I felt guilty. I do not want to hurt you, I don't want to hurt myself, and I don't want to hurt our family. But, then I remembered that I am on a mission to break the cycles of generational trauma so our culture can stop masking pain and suffering in silence. I'm done with that, Brother. I want more for our family, our children and every Little Girl and Little Boy around the world!*

*"I wish we had another chance to have the relationship we truly desired with one another. In a weird way, I feel closer to you than I ever did before. Maybe this book played a part in that. I just wish I could share it with you. I wish you were here!"*

The full weight of grief was now present. Dr. Sharon broke the silence and whispered, *"How do you feel?"*

*"I'm okay,"* I mumbled. Then Dr. Sharon explained something that never crossed my mind.

*"Your brother's life will add to the change in someone else's*

*life because you put it out there. He has a part in helping people get delivered and becoming whole as well. Even in his death, he can help people in a way he wasn't able to while he was living. I think he would be proud of that!"*

Hmmm, I didn't think about it like that! She said exactly what I didn't know I needed to hear. We ended the session and I sat on the edge of my bed basking in the peace and gratitude that settled in my spirit. While I was kind of disappointed that I didn't have the same experience with the Empty Chair Exercise that I did the first time because I didn't feel your presence like I wanted to, I was happy to express what I wanted to say to you for so long. Just as I got up to leave the room, a song dropped in my heart…

*"When peace like a river attendeth my way,*
*When sorrow like sea billows roll,*
*Whatever my lot, thou has taught me to say,*
*It is well, it is well, with my soul."*

Was this you trying to tell me something? Because this song was not just a hymn I remembered, it represented something different, something new. I am well because all is well with us.

It is amazing how situations come full circle and how journeying through a Delabeling Process can make one feel complete. But, complete does not mean finished. No, Dear Brother, I am far from finished. With this book my hope is that other women's identities will be unfolded, healthy boundaries will be set, relationships will be restored, and love for self and others will replace any past label that limits the Dear Reader that holds our book! Yes, I said it! This book is dedicated to you, too, Dear Brother. This is our story and together we will sprinkle hope, restoration, and healing wherever this book goes.

Just know you are always in my heart and forever loved. Rest well, Dear Brother.

**Hey, Dear Reader:** The Delabeling Process is getting down to the nitty gritty and saying "Y.E.S." to the hard stuff. The Empty Chair Process helped me fill the voids and heal the wounded places in my Little Girl and my present self.

Do you feel like you have unresolved business with someone whether they are living or have passed? Is there something you wish you could say to a family member or friend to free yourself from any guilt, shame, or uneasy feeling you have within? What do you need to do to settle the unrest in your spirit?

Emptying your heart with writing a letter or making an audible recording are ways to relieve yourself of any past labels that are not easy to peel off. Like using a scrub brush to scrub food residue from the bottom of a pot, sometimes we have to put some "elbow grease" into getting stubborn labels off.  Imagine leaving the left over particles in the pot ... that could cause mold or bacteria to grow. When you go to cook with that pot the next time the yucky stuff will cook in with the fresh food causing contamination and at worse food poisoning.

You worked so hard up to this point. To continue to live in your "Y.E.S." you have to continue to scrap out anything and everything that tries to stick to you. Cleansing out everything that limits you can liberate a burdened spirit and heal a wounded soul.

### Delabeling Exercise

Write a letter to that person you've been wanting to address for a long time now. You do not have to send it to them, nor do you have to keep the letter. Writing a letter or creating a voice note frees your mind, helps heal pain, releases anger, and creates a nonstick surface for past labels to fall off.

As a way to check in with yourself, write a letter or record yourself as many times as you want to. This exercise is a good way to keep yourself De-labeled, ensuring you continue to journey in your "Y.E.S."

# ACKNOWLEDGMENTS

I AM SO GRATEFUL TO God for the opportunity to share my story with the world in hopes that women like me will experience the greatest sense of freedom through their "Y.E.S."!

To my amazing husband, thank you for your love and support and staying up into the wee-hours of the night to wait for me to come to bed after writing. You are my dream come true. I love doing life with you! To my promise, Kaira, and my blessing, Sean … you two are the joys of my life! Even at a young age, you showed so much compassion when asking me about my book and "you got this, Mom" encouragments. I love you both to the moon and back!

Thank you to my dad, mom, and siblings for the significant parts you've played in making me into the woman I have become today! I love you all! In loving memory of my Big Brother…you are always in my heart.

To my "Crew" thank you for checking in on me and being my biggest supporters. To my bestfriends, Sherria, Myking, and Syreeta, I am so grateful for our bond and sisterhood. You gals ROCK! To Momma D, a.k.a. my angel, words can not express how blessed I am to have you in my life … thanks for being "my person."

I appreciate everyone who is a part of my Fleet of S.H.I.Ps, especially the "Y.E.S."ers in the Say "Y.E.S." Facebook group. Your energy fuels me to keep going. To Dr. Sharon, the Empty Chair Exercise is the catalyst for this book. I am so glad you strongly encouraged me to do it. Thank you for helping me every step of the way on this journey.

To my writing coach Geo, aka Book Doula, I do not think I would have been able to do this without you! I appreicate your words of wisdom, encouragment, and virtual tissues when things got teary … lol. I am also grateful for my FBD Family who I had the pleasure of journeying through this book writing process with. I have gained a family through seven people who were once strangers … you all are stuck with me now J!

Thank you to my editor Jessica Gang, my book cover designer Tri, my photographer, Lashsawn, for my beautiful cover photos, Emily and Cartoon1992 for my Little Girl illustrations, and Chris Derrick for my interior design. You all helped me bring my vision to reality…thank you, "Book Fleet!"

And, to you, Dear Reader, thank you for getting this book. The sky is the limit for you because you said "Y.E.S."!

Lastly, to you, Little Girl, persistance pays off! We are healed! We are whole! We are free!

# ABOUT THE AUTHOR

**VANIA SWAIN** is a mental health counselor, multi-level entrepreneur, certified transformational coach, and founder of "Y.E.S." Coaching Program, LLC, where her signature, Delabeling Process, was developed to help women peel off past limiting labels. She loves to share her story as a transformational message to "Take the Labels Off" and to live life as free as a bird. Becoming an author to help other women is just one of the ways Vania wanted to show her family, friends, and Dear Readers that they, too, can soar to boundless places if they say "Y.E.S." to their dreams.

One of Vania's proudest moments was fulfilling her dream by graduating with a 4.0 GPA and with Phi Chi National Society Honors at the age of forty years old. She's made a lot of choices in life but giving up on this dream was never a choice!

Her and her husband and best friend, Maurice, have been married for seventeen years. They are business partners for their counseling agency, On-Purpose Counseling, LLC. Their two smart and amazing children are the apples of their eye. She and her family reside in South New Jersey.

# AFFIRMATIONS

1. I love and accept myself.
2. I have the capability to reach my goals.
3. I attract what I need.
4. I choose to be proud of myself and how far I have come.
5. Change starts with me. I am a cycle breaker.
6. The world provides endless opportunities for me.
7. I am ready to embrace every challenge, free of self-doubt.
8. I already know exactly what I need to do to achieve success.
9. Creativity is in me. I am turning my ideas into action.
10. I learn something new each day.
11. I will only focus on things I can control such as my actions.
12. I will try something new today.
13. I am strong and confident in my body.
14. My heart is full of courage, kindness, and love.
15. I am thankful for my good health.
16. My body is unique and should not be compared to others.
17. When I take care of my body, my body will take care of me.

18. I define my worth and I am worthy.
19. I trust my intitution and will listen to where it guides me.
20. I am brave when I ask for help.
21. I have a lot to offer the world.
22. I am a magnet for positivity.
23. I am enough because I said so.
24. I desire success.
25. Nothing will stop me from reaching my dreams.
26. I have no room for negativity.
27. Today, I am brimming energy and overflowing with joy.
28. My purpose comes from a place of compassion.
29. Peace and happiness belong to me.
30. I have the strength, the courage, and ability to bounce back.
31. I am enough!
32. My "Y.E.S." makes me free and keeps me limitless.
33. My purpose comes from a place of compassion.
34. Peace and happiness belong to me.
35. I am healed and I am whole.
36. I am writing new chapters to my life's story.
37. I have the strength, the courage, and ability to bounce back.
38. I am enough!
39. My "Y.E.S." makes me free and keeps me limitless.
40. I am living a Delabeled Life!

# BECOME A "Y.E.S."ER

(Bold and courageous women who said, "Y.E.S.")

Speaking and Coaching Opportunities:
For speaking inquires or counseling and coaching opportunities email support@vaniaswain.com.

Other Ways to Join…
Join to receive motivational newsletters:
http://heylittlegirlbook.com/
Say Y.E.S. Facebook Group: https://www.facebook.com/groups/666123827261312

# MENTAL HEALTH RESOURCES

Office on Women's Health

1-800-944-9662

www.womenshealth.gov


Better Help

Individual, Couples, and Teenage Counseling

www.betterhelp.com


Substance Abuse and Mental Health Services

Administration (SAMHSA) National Helpline

External

(1-800-662-HELP (4357)


Y.E.S Coaching Program, coaching@vaniaswain.com

# BOOK SUGGESTIONS

Here are some transformational book suggestions. These authors have been impactful in my journey and are all a part of my Mentor-SHIP!

*Adundance Now* by Lisa Nichols

*Get Over It!* by Iyanla Vanzant

*Limitless* by Jim Kwik

*Becoming* by Michelle Obama

*The Power of Vulnerability* by Brene' Brown

*The Four Agreements* by Don Miguel Ruiz

*Love Without Conditions* by Paul Ferrini

*The Big Leap* by Gay Hendricks

*Girl, Stop Apologizing* by Rachel Hollis

*Believe Bigger* by Marshawn Evan-Daniels

*Geo's Gems* by Geo Derice

*Crushing* by TD Jakes

*Journey to Self-Love* by Melissa Fredericks

*More Than Enough* by Elaine Welteroth

*High Performance Habits* by Brendon Burchard

*Relational Intelligence* by Dr. Dharius Daniels

# REFERENCES


1.  Beyoncé. (2019, July 23). Bigger (Official Audio) [Video]. YouTube. https://www.youtube. com/watch?v=14di5tJxn7c

2.  Borchard, T. J. (2019). The 10 mask we wear. [Web blog post]. Psych Central. Retrieved from https://psychcentral.com/blog/the-10-masks-we-wear/

3.  Brady, M. (1992). *Beyond Survival: A Writing Journey for Healing Childhood Sexual Abuse*. New York, NY: HarperCollins Publishers, Inc.

4.  Brown, Brené. *The Power of Vulnerability*. Narrated by Brené Brown, Audible, 2013. Audiobook.

5.  Delarme, R. (2019). The 10 Mask we wear. Retrieved from https://stillnessinthestorm. com/2019/03/the-10-masks- we-wear/

6.  Fox, J., Mullen, P. R., & Giordano, A. (2017). "Forgiveness, Humility, and Hope: An Interview With Everett L. Worthington Jr." Counseling & Values, 62(1), 11–23. https://doi. org.library.capella.edu/10.1002/cvj.12046

7.  Fredericks, M. (2016), *The Journey to Self-Love*.

United States. Melissa Fredericks

8.  Gaba, S. (2019). "Trauma Bonding, Codependency, and Narcissistic Abuse." [Web blog post]. *Psychology Today*. Retrieved from https://www.psychologytoday.com/us/blog/addiction-and-recovery/201905/trauma-bonding-codependency-and-narcissistic-abuse

9.  Hardy, B. (2015, December 8). "20 Signs you've evolved as a person." [Web blog post]. Retrieved from https://observer.com/2015/12/20-signs-youve-evolved-as-a-person/

10. Hendricks, G. (2009). *The Big Leap*. New York, NY: HarperCollins Publishers, Inc.

11. Hurd, S. A. A. (2018). "7 Subtle Ways Childhood Trauma Affects You When You Are an Adult." [Web blog post]. Retrieved by https://www.learning-mind.com/childhood-trauma-effects/

12. Jakes, T. D. (2019). *Crushing: God Turns Pressure Into Power*. New York, NY. FaithWords/Hachette Book Group.

13. Jeanty, P. A. (2020). *HER*. Retrieved from https://pierrejeanty.com/collections/all-books/products/her

14. John Hopkins Medicine. (n.d.) "Healthy Aging: Forgiveness, Your Health Depends On It." Retrieved from https://www.hopkinsmedicine.org/health/healthy_aging/healthy_connections/

forgiveness-your-health-depends-on-it

15. Kwik, J. (2020). Limitless: Upgrade Your Brain, Learn  Anything Faster, and Unlock Your Exceptional Life. Carlsbad, CA: Hay House,  Inc.

16. Lopez, S. J., Pedrotti, J. T., & Snyder, C. R. (2015). *Positive psychology: The Scientific and Practical Explorations of Human Strengths (3rd ed.).* Thousand Oaks, CA: Sage Publications.

17. Maya, A. (2015). *I Know Why The Caged Bird Sings.* New York, NY: Ballantines Books Mass Market Edition.

18. Mindvalley. (2019, April 3). "The Power of 'I am enough.'" Marissa Peer. [Video]. YouTube. https://www.youtube.com/watch?v=YYE0J-rMj-c

19. Nichols, L. (2009). *No Matter What!: 9 Steps to Living  The Life You Love.* New York, NY: Wellness Group/Hachette Book Group.

20. Obama, M. (2018). *Becoming.* New York, NY: Penguin, Random House.

21. Pharaon, V. "Love Can Be Unconditional, Relationships  Cannot." *Instagram*, August    24, 2020, URL (without//).

22. Ruiz, D. M. (1997). *The Four Agreements: A Toltec Wisdom Book.* San Rafael, CA: Amber-Allen Publishing, Inc.

23. Sanchez, G. M. A., May, R. W., Koutnik, A. P.,

& Fincham, F. D. (2015). "Impact of Negative Affectivity and Trait Forgiveness on Aortic Blood  Pressure and Coronary Circulation." *Psychophysiology*, 52(2), 296–   303. https://doi-org.library.capella.edu/10.1111/psyp.12325

24. Sparks, S. (2015)."The Masks We Wear: 'Imposture Syndrome' and Why We Sometimes Feel Like a Fake." [Web blog post]. *Psychology Today*. Retrieved from https://www.psychologytoday.com/us/blog/laugh-your-way-well-being/201510/the-masks-we-wear

25. Tedx Talks (2016)."The 5 People You Need To Be Happy." Stacey Flowers [Video].YouTube. https://www.youtube.com/watch?v=yZRCF K1n-NM

26. Weir, K. (2017). "Forgiveness Can Improve Mental and Physical Health."American Psychological Association. Retrieved from https://apa.org/monitor/2017/01/ce- corner.aspx

27. White, J. (2020, September 15). "Ultra-Independence is a Trauma Response." Facebook. Retrieved  September 27, 2020,   from https://m.facebook.com/story.php?story_f bid=3  4982120135786017&id=469065889826577

# NOTES:

www.ingramcontent.com/pod-product-compliance
Lightning Source LLC
Chambersburg PA
CBHW022048050726
47591CB00002B/442